Transportation Iss

SUSTAINABLE SUPPLIER MANAGEMENT IN THE AUTOMOTIVE INDUSTRY: LEADING THE 3RD REVOLUTION THROUGH COLLABORATION

TRANSPORTATION ISSUES, POLICIES AND R&D

Public Transit Issues and Developments
Calvin B. Lang (Editor)
2009. 978-1-60692-689-5

Railway Transportation:
Policies, Technology and Perspectives
Nicholas P. Scott (Editor)
2009. 978-1-60692-8639

Yacht Modelling and Adaptive Control
Chengmo Xiao and Sing Kiong Nguang (Authors)
2009. 978-1-60741-430-8

Aeropolitics
Ruwantissa Abeyratne (Author)
2009. 978-1-60876-102-9

High Speed Passenger Rail:
Viability, Challenges and Federal Role
Augelli Biocchetti (Editor)
2010. 978-1-60741-985-3

Wireless Technologies in Intelligent
Transportation Systems
Ming-Tuo Zhou, Yan Zhang
and Laurence T. Yang (Editors)
2010. 978-1-60741-588-6

Automotive Industry: Technical Challenges,
Design Issues and Global Economic Crisis
Gordan A. Maxwell and Stuart K. Drummond (Editors)
2010. 978-1-60876-143-2

Transportation Issues, Policies and R&D

Sustainable Supplier Management in the Automotive Industry: Leading the 3rd Revolution through Collaboration

Mario Binder

and

Ben Clegg

Nova Science Publishers, Inc.

New York

For permission to use material from this book please contact us:
Telephone 631-231-7269; Fax 631-231-8175
Web Site: http://www.novapublishers.com

NOTICE TO THE READER

The Publisher has taken reasonable care in the preparation of this book, but makes no expressed or implied warranty of any kind and assumes no responsibility for any errors or omissions. No liability is assumed for incidental or consequential damages in connection with or arising out of information contained in this book. The Publisher shall not be liable for any special, consequential, or exemplary damages resulting, in whole or in part, from the readers' use of, or reliance upon, this material.

Independent verification should be sought for any data, advice or recommendations contained in this book. In addition, no responsibility is assumed by the publisher for any injury and/or damage to persons or property arising from any methods, products, instructions, ideas or otherwise contained in this publication.

This publication is designed to provide accurate and authoritative information with regard to the subject matter covered herein. It is sold with the clear understanding that the Publisher is not engaged in rendering legal or any other professional services. If legal or any other expert assistance is required, the services of a competent person should be sought. FROM A DECLARATION OF PARTICIPANTS JOINTLY ADOPTED BY A COMMITTEE OF THE AMERICAN BAR ASSOCIATION AND A COMMITTEE OF PUBLISHERS.

Library of Congress Cataloging-in-Publication Data

Binder, Mario.
  Sustainable supplier management in the automotive industry : leading the 3rd revolution through collaboration / Mario Binder, Ben Clegg.
      p. cm.
  Includes bibliographical references and index.
  ISBN 978-1-61668-675-8 (softcover)
  1. Automobile industry and trade. 2. Business logistics. 3. Strategic planning. 4. Business networks. I. Clegg, Ben. II. Title.
  HD9710.A2B526 2010
  629.222068'7--dc22
                                    2010013740

Published by Nova Science Publishers, Inc. † New York

CONTENTS

PREFACE

Global economic pressures have had a dramatic impact on the global automotive industry. It has increased the need for another great automotive revolution. The 1st great revolution was all about 'mass-production'and was principally led by the U.S.. The 2nd great revolution was focused on 'mass-customisation' and was principally led by Japan. The ideas proposed in this book suggest that the European automotive industry will lead the 3rd great automotive revolution; which will probably be achieved via mass-collaboration and sustainable supplier management practices.

This book discusses current trends in the automotive industry, theoretical perspectives about strategic thinking, new case studies and new pragmatic management frameworks. The key messages in this book are that collaboration between car manufacturers and their suppliers need to occur earlier on in the product development process, thinking based on competence rather than cost issues is required, and the creation of value between organisations needs to be rethought. These key factors, along with others explained in the book use the established academic theory, new case studies, methodologies and novel management tools to provide the reader with coping skills and radical insights into how the industry may change over the forth-coming decades. This radical thinking could help pave Europe's way towards successfully leading the 3rd automotive revolution.

This book will be of interest to students, scholars and practitioners of strategic management. It will be particularly interesting to those aiming to influence the future of the automotive industry, and those wishing to learn about innovative supplier management practices.

ACKNOWLEDGEMENTS

Extensive thanks is given to all the companies, interviewees and questionnaire respondents from the German automotive industry who have greatly contributed to the facts and results reported in this book with their expertise. For reasons of ensured confidentiality they remain anonymous.

We would like to thank Aston Business School for supporting the underlying empirical research. Specifically, we would like to acknowledge our colleagues from the Operations and Information Management Research Group for their continuous input and inspirations.

Last but not least, we would like to express our deepest thanks to the editorial team of Nova Science Publishers for their constant support on all sorts of matters.

LIST OF ACRONYMS

AE	Autonomous Enterprise
BMW	Bayrische Motorenwerke
CAD	Computer Aided Design
DC	DaimlerChrysler
DCV	Dynamic Capabilities View
EE	Extended Enterprise
GM	General Motors
GTM	Grounded Theory Method
IMP	Industrial Marketing and Purchasing (Group)
IO	Industrial Organisation
IT	Information Technology
LE	Linked Enterprise
NPD	New Product Development
NVivo	NUD*IST (Nonnumerical Unstructured Data Indexing Searching and Theorising) Vivo
OEM	Original Equipment Manufacturer (car manufacturer)
PDP	Product Development Process
PE	Partner Enterprise
QSR	Qualitative Solutions and Research (International Ltd.)
R&D	Research and Development
RBV	Resource Based View
RDT	Resource Dependency Theory
SCM	Supply Chain Management
SOP	Start of Production
TCE	Transaction Cost Economics
TM	Trademark

TQM	Total Quality Management
U.S.	United States (of America)
USA	United States of America
UK	United Kingdom
VDA	Verband der Automobilindustrie (Association of the German Automotive Industry)
VE	Virtual Enterprise
VIE	Vertically Integrated Enterprise
VW	Volkswagen

## Chapter 1

INTRODUCTION

"If we did not carry in us the basic biological urge to cooperate with our fellow men, we would never have survived as a species" (Morris, 1969; p. 26).

The 1st great automotive revolution in the automotive industry was the move towards mass-production from a craft-based industry (e.g. Fordism); the 2nd great automotive revolution was the move from mass-production towards mass-customisation (e.g. Toyotaism). The 3rd great revolution may be happening right now, and we suspect it is a move towards mass-collaboration. Mass-collaboration is the next logical next step for the automotive industry to take and would build upon the first two revolutions as a matter of necessity. This is because mass-collaboration is essential for the industry to deliver what customers now expect in their vehicles; namely that of low cost, often achieved through mass-production, and high customisation, achieved through mass-customisation. These consumer demands are at conflict with one another in terms of organisational strategy and operational practicalities. Without close and intense collaboration between all types of organisations within the industry, these conflicting demands are unlikely to be able to be met sustainably. We will explore the implications of the 3rd great automotive revolution in this book.

The current global economic crisis is also contributing to the changing ways in which the automotive industry strategises. As rarely does a day go by without news that a major OEM (original equipment manufacturer) such as GM, Chrysler, Toyota, Daimler & Co. has downsized, made huge losses or gone bankrupt. As a result, many workplaces are in jeopardy and political agendas are being reviewed. Some governments have been keen to intervene and support their automotive industries through direct financial packages (e.g. the USA) or other more creative initiatives such as the use of a 'scrapping bonus' when a new car is bought and an old one is scrapped, which was initiated by the German government, and has since been emulated by other European countries (e.g. UK).

However, many people will ask themselves with good reason if pumping billions of Euros into ailing automotive companies hides much more deeper-rooted problems in their underlying processes and business models, that have emerged from gross miss-direction of the industry over recent decades? In our opinion, the current crisis has just accelerated the need for a radical paradigm shift that began some time ago; this is a shift towards smaller and cheaper cars that can be mass customised quickly, use less fuel and can be equipped with alternative propulsion concepts (e.g. hybrid engines etc.); this requires a fundamentally new awareness of the customers and suppliers. This emerging change has temporarily created a strong imbalance within the product portfolios of the OEMs because they have not factored it into their long term production programmes. As a result, capacity problems in the upstream supply chain for producing smaller and cheaper cars will occur even more so than in the past,.Whilst at the same time having over-capacities for cars in the premium segment; this will lead to bottlenecks in material supply in some areas and a loss in turnover and profit in others. Overall, these conditions paint a turbulent and uncertain future for the car industry.

Economic success for the automotive sector, like most others, is based upon a mixture of competitive advantages gained from reducing production costs or increasing innovation, which in turn should result in more attractive value propositions for end customers. This is more likely to occur if reliable production facilities are readily available and innovative thinking in and around new product and process design happens between collaborating organisations. This practice requires a paradigm shift to occur, as managers need to move away from traditional reactive management actions towards more proactive, flexible and sustainable supplier management practices driven by early and intense collaboration. This is what we term the 3rd great revolution in the automotive industry; which is characterised by moving away from adversarial ways of doing business towards mass-collaboration in a post-supply chain era.

However, this shift is difficult to achieve because the main factors emanate from the early stages of the supply process, and so effective sustainable supplier management has to be applied right at the start of the product development process, when strategic sourcing decisions and product and process innovations are taking place. This new way of thinking requires very high levels of foresight and trust between participating organisations, which is difficult to achieve, especially in turbulent economic situations.

For instance, Audi has demonstrated that more effective group-wide capacity planning and supplier management can be achieved if their key suppliers are included in their initial planning and coordination phase of new product development. This means that potential capacity problems can be identified earlier on, resulting in better programme stability and a more economic supply of materials (Krog and Lochmahr, 2006). However, newly emerging cost cutting initiatives, which have been initiated in response to the current economic crisis, show that many automotive companies are still not focused on long term sustainable supplier management practices. For industry insiders this already indicates a fallback to the once adversarial Lopez era 15-20 years ago in which car manufacturers (e.g. the OEMs) gained significant cost savings at the expense of their suppliers which led to deep-rooted mistrust between manufacturers and suppliers.

Hence, it is vital that the integrative and collaborative aspects of automotive development are visible accounted for and measured appropriately so that companies do not continuously fall into the trap of making poor reactive decisions in response to bottleneck crises or cost-cutting tactics for short-term process improvements. We believe that a more intense collaboration between car manufacturers and their suppliers earlier in the product development process is necessary. Based on *competence* rather than *cost* issues, as well as the right proportion of value adding activities devolved towards suppliers, which will encourage overall long term time-scale reduction and greater innovation. Which in turn, may finally realise the 5-day-car vision from order to delivery (Parry and Graves, 2008), and hence lead the way towards the 3rd revolution.

However, none of the existing approaches to supplier management appears entirely adequate for managers who face the practical problems of creating and operating sustainable supplier management. The collaborative framework presented in this book aims to overcome this deficiency by supporting managers in their strategic and operative decision making process within the context of inter-organisational collaboration for sustainable supplier management.

In Chapter 2 the term collaborative economy and its meaning are introduced. We argue that many industries move away from vertical integration towards virtual integration; which not only leads to a rethinking of the economic model of an organisation, but also to a change in focus from the organisational level to the inter-organisational level in a post-supply chain era.

In Chapter 3 the need for sustainable management of R&D projects, based on collaboration within automotive supply networks, is explained. It is shown that an increasing percentage of competitive value in the car industry is generated by suppliers through their innovative power which forces the OEMs to adopt innovative tactics for dealing with suppliers in R&D projects.

In Chapter 4 the current state of knowledge on inter-firm relationship governance is investigated from a theoretical point of view, and the topic is embedded in a wider interdisciplinary body of knowledge which includes Organisation Economics, Strategic Management, Organisation Science, Industrial Marketing and Supply Chain Management.

Chapter 5 describes the research objectives, point of departure and research approach of a detailed empirical study on inter-firm R&D collaboration conducted in the German automotive industry. A Grounded Theory Method approach was adopted using semi-structured interviews, self-administered questionnaires and focus groups. The chapter concludes with the novel findings that were gained during this three year in-depth study based on the detailed analysis and codification of the data. Findings show that current practice in the German automotive industry does not apply mechanisms and concepts for sustainable inter-firm collaboration although ironically it is actually considered necessary to achieve sustainable competitive success.

Chapter 6 introduces a novel competence based contingency framework for the sustainable governance of inter-organisational R&D relationships within the automotive industry, which is referred to as *Collaborative Enterprise Governance*. The elements of the concept are described and a step-by-step approach for its application is given to support automotive managers who may wish to practice it.

In Chapter 7 discusses the practical implications of the framework's application for sustainable supplier management. Recommendations for OEMs and suppliers are given on how to lead the 3rd revolution in the car industry in order to support the creation of a distinct European governance model that is based on partnership-focused collaborative relationships.

In the final Chapter 8 the main aspects of the previous chapters are summarised, it also explains the limitations of the novel concept, as well as ideas for future research that seem vital for an automotive industry in crisis.

Chapter 2

THE COLLABORATIVE ECONOMY

"The greatest change in corporate culture, and the way business is being conducted, may be the accelerating growth of relationships based not on ownership, but on partnership" (Drucker, 1996).

New industrial circumstances, such as hypercompetition (D'Aveni, 1994; Ilinitch *et al.*, 1996) and clockspeed (Fine, 1998), are leading to a vertical disintegration or disaggregation of companies and a stronger involvement in activities that are outside their traditional company boundaries (Gittell and Weiss, 2004; Miles and Snow, 1986). In order to adapt to the resulting changes in nature and locus of competition in a globalised 'information age' (Sampler, 1998) connections, i.e. strategic relationships nurtured by collaboration, with specialised companies are crucial for the '21st century corporation' (Davidow and Malone, 1992) or 'fifth generation organisations' (Savage, 1990).[1] These ideas all endorse the increasing need for alliance between organisations. Gulati (1998) defines alliances as:

"voluntary arrangements between firms involving exchange, sharing, or co-development of products, technologies, or services" (p. 293).

Similarly, Das and Teng (2000) view alliances as:

"voluntary cooperative inter-firm agreements aimed at achieving competitive advantage for the partners" (p. 33).

---

[1] The underlying philosophy of work specialisation is rooted in the original work of Adam Smith (1776), and later Charles Babbage (1835) who transferred the idea from manual work to intellectual work.

As such they can be subtly distinguished from joint ventures (JVs). Kumar and Seth, (1998) define JVs as:

"independent organisations formed by the pooling of resources and sharing of equity by two or more firms".

Thereby, partnerships, whether alliances or JVs can provide access to specific assets and resources an organisation does not possess or cannot develop itself and can also provide the opportunity to leverage its existing capabilities into more significant strategic positions via the 'relationship capital' generated through collaboration without further investment (Hamel, 1991; Hamel *et al.*, 1989). Partnerships are sometimes considered to be the 'supply chain's lifeblood' (Liker and Choi, 2004) or 'Marketing's fifth 'P''[2] (Dull *et al.*, 1995) and should become routine for many companies, rather than an optional choice for organisations (Hamel *et al.*, 1989), as "finding a strong partner to complement an area of weakness gives an organisation an island of stability in a turbulent world" (McFarlan and Nolan, 1995; p. 11).

Over the past years, collaboration with partners outside the traditional organisational boundaries has become a more integral part of business life, and is now amongst the most dramatic and visible manifestations of new strategies for sustainable competitive advantage at a corporate level (e.g. Dyer, 1996a and 2000; Dyer and Ouchi, 1993; Dyer and Singh, 1998; Hines, 1994; Kanter, 1994). IBM's recent Global CEO Study (2006), conducted with 765 business leaders of 20 different industries, revealed that almost 40% of respondents consider business partners to be the most significant source of innovation; and an even higher percentage (75%) of respondents thinks that collaboration and partnering are of great importance (IBM, 2006).

Inter-organisational collaboration is justified by serving as a 'competitive weapon' that adds value to the organisations and their customers, e.g. improving performance, delivering savings, and allowing focus on core activities by engaging in partnerships and cooperation with various players (Drago, 1997). The combined effects of these factors have stimulated the emergence of a new business model in which competitive advantage is based on the development of relationships with partners (Hamel *et al.*, 1989; Walters, 2004). The success of the resulting webs of complex and dynamic relationships (Harland and Knight, 2001) depends on the ability of the partner companies to intermediate their internal core competencies into collaborating

---

[2] The four other marketing "P's" are considered to be Product, Price, Place and Promotion.

companies' value streams and simultaneously strategically outsource their own peripheral activities to companies that can perform them quicker, cheaper, and more effectively (Hakansson and Snehota, 1989; Quinn and Hilmer, 1994). In other words, the peripheral activities of one company must be complemented by core competencies of a partner company within a collaborative venture.

In this context, the traditional market (buy) and hierarchy (make) dichotomy represent endpoints on a continuum of inter-organisational strategies. This could mislead managers and researchers to overlook the possibilities of intermediate alliance or partnership strategies (hybrids) as a sustainable source of competitive advantage. An alliance may combine the advantages of vertical integration and transactional contracts, whilst overcoming some of their disadvantages (Dyer and Hatch, 2004; Jarillo, 1988; Jones et al., 1997; Thorelli, 1986). However, there is also a 'dark side' to close relationships, characterised by opportunistic behaviour of the partners, which are a degree of lock-in due to a lack of alternatives and predicable path dependency in relationship behaviour, etc. (Anderson and Jap, 2005; Bruner and Spekman, 1998; Rossetti and Choi, 2005). Companies need to be aware of this and should not only focus on their internal transformation activities but also on inter-organisational structures, processes and transactions, because collaboration is particularly difficult when appropriate internal processes and structures are not present (Chesbrough and Teece, 1996).

This has led to an increased focus on new value structures, beyond linear value chains towards more hub and network-based structures (Cousins and Crone, 2003). In other words, the previous relatively simple vertical business-to-business relationships, conducted at arms length, are becoming embedded in complex inter-organisation networks (Harland et al., 2003). Similarly, Bowersox et al. (2000) and Hamel and Prahalad (1994) acknowledged that many industries move away from vertical integration toward virtual integration. This leads to the rethinking of the economic model of a traditional organisational form, from firm-centric, that is focused on transformation within firm boundaries, to network centric, that is focused on interaction across firm boundaries. This is shown in Figure 1. The 1st revolution saw a change in the scale of economies from a craft based industry to a mass-production set-up. Both of these practices still relied heavily on the single individual firm operating independently. The 2nd revolution saw a move from mass-production to mass customisation; it gave a dramatic increase in the economies of scope, which was achieved through more outsourcing and developing long chains of suppliers. The 3rd revolution has been instigated by the industry searching for a sustainable way to practice both mass-production and mass customisation.

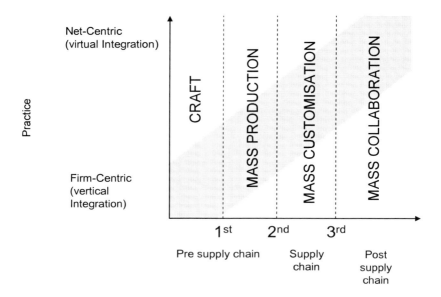

Figure 1. Changing Practice in the Automotive Industry: Eras and Revolutions.

The emerging network structures based on virtual integration are not only a hybrid form in the continuum of a firm's inter-organisational governance strategies but are also an intermediary between the industrial micro (firm) and macro (industrial sector) level (Thorelli, 1986; Madhavan *et al.*, 1998). Network or increasingly virtual organisational structures are therefore becoming more significant as an organisational form (Ketchen and Giunipero, 2004). Camps *et al.* (2004) even go a step further by creating the terminology of 'chain and network science' to stress the importance of the network phenomenon as an emerging science.

The underlying change in analysis focus is particularly important when considering the fact that the competition of whole networks or supply chains, rather than single firms, is the central tenet in modern supply chain management (Christopher, 1998; Gomes-Casseres, 1994); and the partnership with the most efficient and effective structures and processes will ultimately dominate the market and its competitors. For that reason, the central unit of analysis in the strategic management of supply relationships has to shift from the organisational level to the inter-organisational level and focus on how groups of organisational compete against other groups of organisations (Bettis, 1998; Harland, 1996; MacBeth and Ferguson, 1994; Wood and Gray, 1991). Ultimately, this involves the sustainable[3] management of relationships and partnerships based on successful inter-organisational collaboration; which requires a shift in management thinking and business focus (Kopczak and Johnson, 2003).

2.1. SUMMARY

Many industries move away from vertical integration towards virtual integration leading to a rethinking of the economic model of an organisation from firm-centric, that is focused on transformation within firm boundaries, to network centric that is focused on interaction across firm boundaries. Over recent decades the automotive industry has undergone a number of revolutions and we are now experiencing the 3rd great revolution where the industry needs to practice *sustainable* mass-production and mass-customisation. This is bringing the industry into the era of mass-collaboration. Failure to do this is likely to result in automotive companies operating at a loss, having over capacity and lagging behind in innovation.

The governance of the newly emerging inter-company relationships can be understood by knowing whom to include in the network, and managing the complex nexus of relationships that emerges. This, however, requires a paradigm shift in management thinking and business focus from the organisational level to the inter-organisational level. It is therefore essential that strategists understand the theoretical building blocks of inter-organisational relationship governance in order to facilitate better decision making and supplier management practice.

---

[3] Sustainability refers to the fact that competing inter-firm relationships cannot adopt one's superior capability attributes (Coyne, 1986).

Chapter 3

THE NEED FOR SUSTAINABLE INTER-ORGANISATIONAL R&D COLLABORATION IN THE CAR INDUSTRY

"The automotive industry is at the edge of a third revolution: the breaking of its traditional industrial model" (Managing R&D Director, System Supplier).

Over the next years there will be a continuous transformation process in the automotive industry contributing to a 3rd revolution. (Jürgens, 2004; Voss, 1995). This will require a fundamental rethinking of current business strategies and industrial models. The 3rd revolution will be predominantly characterised by mass-collaboration across firms in the industry. It will be characterised by moving away from the traditional adversarial and contractual model towards a partnership and relational model; this practice will need to be extended to all key players in the automotive industry. We believe that this time Europe (especially Germany) will take the lead in driving this 3rd revolution. From the automotive triad (U.S., Japan, Europe) the U.S. drove the 1st revolution and Japan drove the 2nd revolution. But based on the restructuring of its automotive and supplier industry towards the end of the 1990s, Europe has already embarked on its journey towards the post-supply chain era.

Europe's automotive industry restructuring has endeavoured to preserve competitiveness through the development of specific capabilities related to innovativeness and inter-organisational collaboration (Gottschalk, 2001): "If the future lies in the increased specialisation of [and collaboration between] actors in the value chain, the European automotive industry seems to be specifically well positioned in terms of structures and capabilities" (Jürgens, 2004; p. 132).

Nevertheless, evidence (e.g. A.T. Kearney, 2003) shows that there is still a long way to go for the European automotive industry to be truly sustainable. The implementation of a 'European model' implies the redefinition and restructuring of the industry, moving away from the image of the OEM dominated linear tiered pyramid to the image of networks of partners integrating specific and complementary competencies, in which suppliers will exploit the value of increasing modularity[4] whilst value of orchestration through the focus on product planning, design and marketing will create the modern management approach of the OEMs (Bullinger et al., 2004; Doran, 2003; Dudenhöffer, 2002; Jürgens, 2004).

3.1. GOVERNANCE MODELS IN THE AUTOMOTIVE INDUSTRY

Over time, two contrasting models for characterising the relationships between buyers and suppliers in the automotive industry have emerged: the contractual and the relational model. The contractual model is characterised by adversarial relationships that aim at maximising ones own power position; the relational model involves high levels of collaboration and information exchange between the partners. Firms in the Western automotive industry (particularly U.S. based firms) have traditionally been located within the contractual model, whilst Japanese companies have been more closely related to the relational model (Dyer et al., 1998; Singh et al., 2005). However, this ignores hybrid models which suggest that the 'European model' is moving towards partnerships in the automotive industry. Three different generic approaches towards inter-firm relationship governance in the automotive industry can be identified as shown in Table 1.

---

[4] According to a study, modules and systems accounted for 22%, standards parts and components for 70%, and raw materials 8% of the total supply for European car manufacturers in 1993. In 2000 these proportions have already changed to 43% for modules and systems, 50% for standard parts and components, and 7% for raw materials with a tendency of extrapolating the trend (A.T. Kearney, 2003).

Table 1. Comparison between U.S., European and Japanese governance models (based on Cousins and Stanwix, 2001; Dyer and Ouchi, 1993; Dyer et al., 1998)

Aspect	U.S. adversarial model	European partnership model	Japanese relational model
Sourcing strategy	Parallel sourcing with multiple partners Traditional commodity purchasing (contractual)	Dual / single sourcing Towards strategic sourcing	Sole / single sourcing Strategic sourcing (partnership)
Contracting	Short-term contracts Less formalised (flexible) Price focused	Towards longer-term contracts Less formalised based on Service Level Agreements Technology and innovation focused for critical components, price focused for standard parts	Long-term contracts Formalised (fixed) Quality and delivery focused
Supplier involvement	Low supplier involvement Constant search for new suppliers Involving suppliers as late as possible	High involvement of system and module suppliers Basic supply base and variation for peak volumes Increasingly involving suppliers at early product development stages	High supplier involvement Suppliers chosen for vehicle lifetime Involving suppliers as early as possible
Supplier management	Arms length relationship Single functional interface (sales to purchasing) Self-centred focus on own manufacturing lines	Increasingly relational model Multiple functional interfaces Mainly self-centred with focus on some big system suppliers	Trusting partnership with financial stakes Multiple functional interfaces (R&D to R&D, R&D to sales, sales to purchasing, etc.) Holistic approach to entire business system including supplier
R&D collaboration	Minimal sharing of technical and cost information Sporadic and problem driven communication OEM determines product specifications	Intensive sharing of technical know how but little cost information Mainly problem driven communication Joint product specification for parts with critical supplier know how	Intensive sharing of technical and cost information Frequent and planned communication Joint product specification

However, the boundaries between the models in Table 1 are becoming increasingly blurred and should be considered to be a continuum of approaches and strategies. For example, due to years of recession the Japanese *keiretsus* seem to have allowed more open competition in their relationships (Lamming, 2000; Zirpoli and Caputo, 2002) and therefore are moving closer to the European model. In Europe, German volume manufacturers such as Volkswagen (VW) or Opel (GM) are closer to the U.S. model; premium manufacturers such as AUDI and Porsche are closer to the Japanese-European model; whilst OEMs such as BMW and Daimler seem to be centred in the hybrid European model. Similar trends are revealed by Zirpoli and Caputo (2002) for the Italian automotive industry.

3.2. PRODUCT DEVELOPMENT AND R&D COLLABORATION AS CRITICAL SUCCESS FACTORS

The overall success of a (car) brand depends on its value to the customer which is determined by a multiplicity of factors such as product quality, price, variety, safety, after sales service, etc. Barwise and Meehan (2004) call these 'generic category benefits'. They argue that most companies are too focused on their differentiation activities and thereby forget or neglect to satisfy their customers with products and services that simply provide better generic category benefits. In times of economic crisis it can be expected that these basic customer needs, and factors such as price and quality get even more important.

However, generalisations made from Barwise and Meehan's position need to be kept in check; as it has to be observed that this strategy works well for cars in lower and middle segments but not so well for car manufacturers possessing a premium or luxury image as many of the German OEMs do. Hence, even a 120% fulfilment of generic category benefits does not automatically create a desirable and highly emotional car. This can be underpinned by Lexus' current underperformance on the highly competitive German premium market compared to Toyota's success story in the midsize segments in the rest of the world (Koehler, 2006). In 2003 Toyota only sold around 2,500 Lexus in Germany (Katzensteiner, 2004). In the premium product segments especially, the degree of quality and innovation and the country of origin are especially decisive for the customers' purchase decision (Lamming *et al.*, 2000; Proff, 2000). Hence, premium OEMs of the German automotive industry, such as AUDI, BMW, Mercedes and Porsche, can only gain and maintain a sustainable competitive success by innovation, quality and an acceptable price. The importance of innovation for economic growth is well established (Schumpeter, 1934; and later Drucker, 1985).

In addition, cars involve complex design and engineering skills that can often no longer be achieved by individual companies on their own but are produced through multi-level 'innovation networks' of specialists with complementary competencies (Bullinger et al., 2004; Lamming et al., 2000; Quinn, 2000). This trend has been identified by many studies (which includes Becker and Dietz, 2004; Fritsch and Lukas, 2001; Miotti and Sachwald, 2003; Von Corswant and Fredriksson, 2002) showing that firms in R&D (research and development) intensive industries are increasingly relying on (virtual) partnerships with external suppliers; not only for manufacturing and production but also for product development and innovative activities. This fundamentally alters the view on the automotive product life cycle. As opposed to the past where efficient production processes and outsourcing of manufacturing determined the competitiveness of a car via its price; nowadays innovation, design and quality are increasingly important and need to be built into the product together with specialised suppliers during the development and R&D phase of the lifecycle (Dudenhöffer, 2002).

Based on their core competencies, value focus and contribution suppliers can be allocated to six basic strategic role models in a restructured supplier industry (Jürgens, 2004): *engineering service providers* specialising in product development and design activities (e.g. IVM, EDAG, Bertrandt, etc.); *part and component suppliers* providing high technology and innovation expertise on specific standard parts and components (e.g. Meritor, Nedschroeff, Mahle, Stabilus, etc.); *module suppliers* and *system suppliers* specialising in the integration of parts and components to supply whole modules and systems (e.g. Hella, Siemens VDO, Bosch, Edscha, Valeo, Johnson Controls, Visteon, etc.); *logistics and assembly service providers* focusing on low value added assembly and just in time delivery services (e.g. Scherm Group, Faurecia, etc.); *prime contractors* or *system integrators* providing total process support including sub-supplier management and engineering capabilities for developing and manufacturing whole car series (e.g. Magna, Karmann, Bertone, Valmet, etc.). This is illustrated in Figure 2 which shows the various players (including OEM and suppliers), their value contribution, competencies and interrelationships.

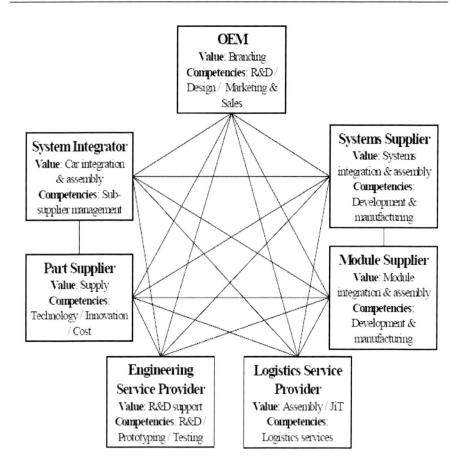

Figure 2. Network of specialists for product development in the automotive industry (adapted from Jürgens, 2000).

However, the restructuring of the industrial landscape in the German automotive industry has led to tensions between OEMs and suppliers in a vicious circle of 'hostile' competition resulting in isolation of the players and a mutual blame culture based on irreversible know-how shift from OEMs to suppliers (sometimes referred to as 'hollowing out'; Becker and Zirpoli, 2003), increasing quality problems in car development and production, and a further consolidation of actors in the supplier industry. For example, a study by Mercer Management Consulting (2004) estimates that from the current 5,500 suppliers around 2,500-3,000 will disappear from the market by 2015 with the top 20 suppliers accounting for approximately 50% of the total OEM supply (currently 27%). Similarly, only seven to ten of the current 12 independent global car manufacturers will be left to compete.

In this respect, recent developments of some OEMs in the German automotive industry (mainly premium manufacturers) show the adoption of more strategic sourcing policies towards collaborative partnerships and active supply management based on long-term R&D decision giving a stronger strategic focus on core competencies in order to cope with the emerging challenges of industrial change (Wolters and Schuller, 1997). However, other OEMs and big suppliers (mainly volume manufacturers) continue the trend of excessive outsourcing of ever larger performance packages to external suppliers in order to cut down R&D and production costs. This can be confirmed with results from a Mercer study (Mercer Management Consulting, 2004) revealing that mass producers especially (e.g. VW, GM, Ford, etc.) are further decreasing their own overall added-value in product development and production, whereas premium manufacturers (e.g. AUDI, BMW, Porsche, Mercedes, etc.) are increasing their value added through brand defining and differentiating components. This is shown in Figure 3.

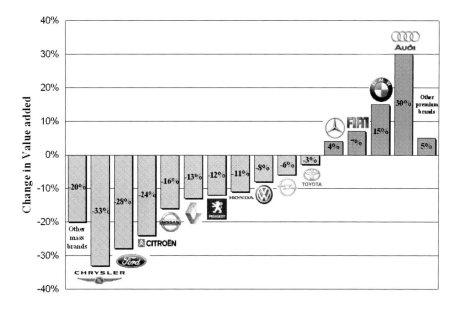

Figure 3. Percentage of change in value added for selected OEMs from 2002 until 2015 (Source: Mercer Management Consulting, 2004).

This is also supported by Dudenhöffer (2003) who claims that most innovations in car development stem from the suppliers (see Figure 4), which partially explains why car development and production is moving from the car manufacturers (OEMs) towards their suppliers (see Figure 5).

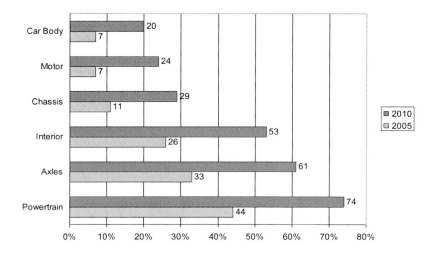

Figure 4. Value-added by suppliers in car development (Source: Arthur D. Little, 2005).

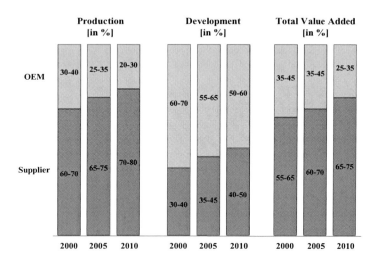

Figure 5. Value-added shifts between OEMs and suppliers in product development and production (adapted from Roland Berger Strategy Consultants, 1999).

Therefore, the development of successful inter-organisational collaboration becomes crucial (Hurmelinna *et al.*, 2002; Morton *et al.*, 2006); particularly as there is an increasing amount of electronic and mechatronic content in cars being delivered by key suppliers (e.g. power train components in Figure 4); this is believed to be about 40% of the total vehicle cost by 2010 (VDA, 2006). Therefore, sustainable competitive success will require OEMs to involve the right suppliers for each specific task of product development and establish systematic linkages with them to ensure effective and efficient collaborative ventures. This is necessary because:

- during the product development stages strategic supply and sourcing decisions are made that influence and determine the collaborative relationship structure between the partners in the supply network (A.T. Kearney, 2004) and hence the probability for bottlenecks in material supply at production stages.
- R&D and product development are key value drivers for competitive advantage of an automotive company (and the whole alliance) based on the deployment of innovative capabilities and competencies (Harmsen *et al.*, 2000; Prajogo and Sohal, 2006).
- during the product development stages most errors are built into the products and processes which affect the competitiveness of the company and the collaborative venture via the generic category benefits identified by Barwise and Meehan (2004) (Jahn, 1988; Rommel *et al.*, 1994). This is shown in Figure 6.

Hence, product development and more general R&D management is arguably the most important part of the automotive product lifecycle because it determines the overall competitiveness of the car. In Figure 7 the main aspects characterising the product development process[5] in the automotive industry are summarised including the major activities at each of the main stages (product planning, concept design, pre-series design, series design and series production), their critical success factors and major decision gates are shown along a monthly time scale during the development process. In the literature these stages are also sometimes referred to as the initial stage, concept stage,

---

[5] In alignment with Ulrich and Eppinger (1995), R&D or product development is generally described as the sequence of steps or activities that a company employs to conceive design and commercialise a product or service. Joint R&D can be described as the jointly agreed conduction of research and development for a definite technology between two or more companies without equity involvement (Chiesa et al., 2000).

detail engineering stage and process engineering stage/product introduction
(e.g. Hauschildt, 2004); other similar models can for example be found in
Ulrich and Eppinger (1995) and Mikkola (2003).

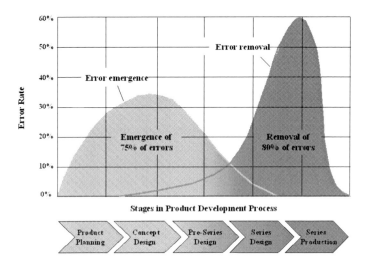

Figure 6. Error emergence and removal in the R&D process (based on Jahn, 1988).

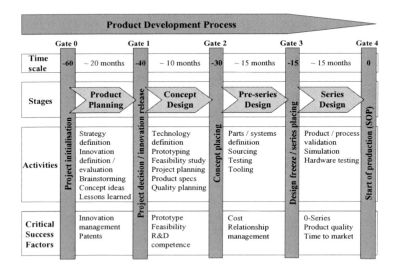

Figure 7. Product development as a stage gate process.

Research also shows that a lack of quality focus during the design process leads to dysfunctional supply chains resulting in an increased number of product recalls (Bates *et al.*, 2007) and expensive rework in downstream production processes (Love *et al.*, 1999).

3.3. SUMMARY

It is evident from current literature that the full range of skills needed to develop innovative and high quality cars is not often in existence under a single roof. OEMs mainly possess strong brand management, design capabilities and the link to the end customer, whereas suppliers have specialised knowledge in technologies, parts and components. Hence, sustainable competitive success will require OEMs to involve the right suppliers for each specific task of product development and establish systematic linkages with them, whilst simultaneously ensuring the effectiveness and efficiency of the collaborative venture. The necessity for more effective and sustainable collaboration between OEMs and suppliers is now more important than ever, especially in the areas of R&D, product development and innovation (Calabrese, 2001). At the same time the establishment of intensive collaboration culture for information and know-how exchange between OEMs and suppliers to create a win-win situation, is one of the greatest challenges in inter-organisational collaboration and sustainable supplier management. Despite these facts, useful validated models, guidelines and frameworks to support practitioners in their strategic decision making about sustainable supplier management and inter-organisational R&D, are still missing.

## Chapter 4

THEORETICAL PERSPECTIVES OF INTER-ORGANISATIONAL RELATIONSHIP GOVERNANCE

"The development of collaborative relationships has been a challenge for mankind throughout history" (Price, 1996; p. 103).

Practical examples of inter-organisational relationships based on inter-organisational governance forms and structures are scattered all over the industrial world. Table 2 lists some potentially interesting cases organised by industry.

Table 2. Selected industrial examples on inter-organisational relationship in the literature

Industry	Literature
Aerospace	Boardman and Clegg (2001), Graham and Ahmed (2000), Morton et al. (2006)
Biotech	Chiesa and Toletti (2004), Hakansson et al. (1993), Powell (1998), Powell at al. (1996), Weisenfeld et al. (2001)
Computer	Baldwin and Clark (1997), Eisenhardt and Tabrizi (1995), Magretta (1998)
Construction	Briscoe (2001), Eccles (1981), Kornelius and Wamelink (1998), Usdiken et al. (1988)

Table 3. Main terms used in inter-organisational relationship literature (see Binder and Clegg, 2007)

Terms used to describe the structural form of an inter-firm relationship	
Terms	Authors
Quasi Firm	Eccles (1981) Luke et al. (1989)
Strategic Network Dynamic Network Project Network	Gulati et al. (2000) Jarillo (1988) Sydow (1992)
Industrial District	Ellegaard et al. (2003)
Clan Keiretsu	Ouchi (1980) Dyer (1996b)
Virtual Corporation / Organisation	Byrne and Brandt (1993) Davidow and Malone (1992) Chesbrough and Teece (1996)
Holonic Organisation / Network	McHugh et al. (1995) Walters (2004)
Supply Network	Cousins and Crone (2003) Lamming et al. (2000) Mills et al. (2004)
Virtual Enterprise	Martinez et al. (2001) Mintzberg et al. (1998)
Extended Enterprise	Boardman and Clegg (2001) Davis and Spekman (2003) Kanter (1999)
Collaborative / networked enterprise	Bititci et al. (2004) Noori and Lee (2004)
Lean enterprise Vertically Integrated enterprise	Binder and Clegg (2006) Womack and Jones (1994)
Extraprise	Karlsson (2003)
Hub firm Focal firm Core firm	Dyer and Hatch (2004) Gulati et al. (2000) Harland and Knight (2001) Nassimbeni (1998)
Architect Designer Integrator	Boardman and Clegg (2001) Mills et al. (2004) Snow et al. (1992) Walters (2004)
Network Manager Project Manager	Harland and Knight (2001) Martinez et al. (2001)
Broker Orchestrator Navigator	Karlsson (2003) Miles and Snow (1986) Snow et al. (1992)
Captain Leader Convenor	Johnsen et al. (2000) Ritter and Gemünden (2003)

It has to be observed that within these industrial examples and the wider literature on inter-firm relationships no consistency in terminology is evident on describing the governance structure of an inter-organisational relationship and for identifying its most strategically influential member. An overview of the most common terms used in the inter-firm relationship literature is provided in Table 3.

However, while the forms and labels for these inter-organisational relationships differ, Nassimbeni (1998) identifies three basic characteristics that inter-organisational relationships have in common:

- They are formed by two or more firms (separate legal entities) leading to a voluntary exchange relationship.
- The mechanism used to govern these transactional exchanges is some form of relational contract that usually departs from economic motives and becomes socially embedded over time.
- Between the parties in the relationship dynamic forms of communication and coordination are used in order to synchronise the partners' activities to the whole relationship that ultimately enables the adaptability of the relationship to exogenous and endogenous contingencies.

In other words, "they all describe the phenomenon whereby the role of a tightly integrated hierarchy is supplanted by 'loosely coupled' networks of organisational actors" (Schilling and Steensma, 2001). However, it is *not* our aim to establish the differences between these types and terms but to emphasise the fact that many studies overlook the potential of a cross-fertilisation of theoretical perspectives for developing well grounded theories on inter-organisational relationship governance.

4.1. STATE OF KNOWLEDGE ON INTER-ORGANISATIONAL RELATIONSHIP GOVERNANCE

The main population or *lebensraum* (Vastag and Montabon, 2002) for relevant literature on inter-firm relationships can be clustered into five disciplinary groups:

(i)   General & Strategic Management
(ii)   Management Science
(iii)   Operations & Supply Management
(iv)   Technology & Innovation Management
(v)   Marketing Management

Within these five disciplinary groups we conducted a systematic and structured literature review into the following four major themes in the period from 2000 until 2007 based on 40 relevant journals. These themes were:

(i)   building and developing inter-organisational relationships (i.e. partner selection, evaluation, integration)
(ii)   managing inter-organisational relationships (i.e. coordination, collaboration, communication)
(iii)   performance impacts and benefits of inter-organisational relationships (i.e. competitive advantage, learning etc.)
(iv)   specific studies of inter-organisational relationships in the automotive industry.

As a result, 160 articles were identified that deemed relevant in terms of one or more of the four themes in the context of inter-organisational relationship governance. Each of the 160 publications was then analysed and categorised regarding:

•   focus and contribution
•   unit of analysis
•   theoretical perspective
•   methodology used.

Table 4 highlights the most significant and representative contributions.

Similar, but less comprehensive and contemporary reviews of inter-firm relationship (governance) can be found in the literature (e.g. Chen and Paulraj, 2004; Cousins, 2002; Gulati, 1998; Ireland *et al.*, 2002, Johnsen *et al.*, 2000; Olsen and Ellram, 1997a).

The detailed analysis revealed that many studies on inter-organisational relationship governance take an isolated view of single theoretical concepts and neglect the necessity for using a multi-perspective approach although this is widely called for by the literature. Moreover, most studies not only take an isolated view of an exogenous or endogenous position, but also mainly focus on the most common conceptual representatives within these streams, such as Transaction Cost Economics (Coase, 1937; Williamson, 1975) and Resource Based View (Barney, 1991; Wernerfelt, 1984). Thereby, these studies overlook the potential of less commonly used concepts, such as Resource Dependency Theory (Pfeffer and Salancik, 1978) or Complex Adaptive Systems (Kauffman, 1993), that might provide valuable and fruitful insights into the governance of inter-organisational relationships (Parkhe *et al.*, 2006).

Moreover, only few scholarly contributions consider the scenario of network vs. network (or chain vs. chain) rather than firm vs. firm. Although inter-organisational relationships are essentially dyadic exchanges, to understand them greater, attention must be directed to the context in which these dyadic relationships exist (Gulati, 1998). Hence, if research is to act as a guide to practice, inter-organisational relationships have to be studied in situ as dyadic buyer-supplier practices in a wider network context. This is a rather neglected view on inter-organisational relationships within the existing literature. In addition, much knowledge on the nature of inter-organisational relationships remains either unexplored or is not supported by reliable empirical evidence (Goffin *et al.*, 2006). This can be explained by the lack of qualitative theory building research on the topic (Handfield and Melnyk, 1998) and hence the necessity for more exploratory research that proposes models and frameworks that can be further tested and modified (Burgess *et al.*, 2006; Olsen and Ellram, 1997a). This is summarised in Table 5.

Taken together, only five of the "network" papers consider empirical evidence, and none of these develops theory using a multi-perspective approach. For example, adopting a knowledge-based view as core theoretical viewpoint within the in-depth case study of Toyota, Dyer and Nobeoka (2000) find that a network with its greater diversity in knowledge is more effective than the single individual firm at the generation, transfer and recombination of knowledge. Bititci *et al.* (2003) similarly focus on one single case study to demonstrate the validity of their developed collaborative architecture for extended enterprises. Using competence theory as main building block they argue for the necessity of a meta-level management process for this architecture in order to create and sustain competitive advantage for collaborative systems. Noori and Lee (2004) investigate product development processes within networks of organisations from a social network point of view.

Table 4. Significant scholarly contributions on inter-firm relationships

Theme	Author(s)	Focus of study / contribution	Unit of analysis	Theoretical perspective	Applied methodology
Building and developing inter-organisational relationships (supplier selection, evaluation, involvement, segmentation, etc.)	Anderson et al. (1994)	Argue that dyadic relationships have to be built within the context of the business network in which the relationships take place	Dyad	Social network theory	Validity assessment
	Bensaou (1999)	A portfolio of relationships is necessary to be adaptive to product and market characteristics	Buyer firm	Contingency theory; Portfolio modelling	Questionnaire survey
	Das et al. (2006)	Argues for an optimal level of supplier integration that leads to maximal performance through the configuration of internal and external integration practices	Buyer firm	Contingency theory	Questionnaire survey/Interviews/ Correlation and regression analysis
	Fine (1998 and 2000)	Develops framework for strategic sourcing under banner of three dimensional concurrent engineering (3-DCE) combining product, process and supply chain issues	Buyer firm	SCM	Conceptual / Case applications
	Hallikas et al. (2002)	Suggests a partner portfolio matrix based on the current transactional effectiveness and the future potential value of the partner	Buyer firm	Contingency theory	Conceptual
	Miotti and Sachwald (2003)	Argues that the selection of partners for R&D collaboration mainly depends on the possession of complementary resources	Buyer firm	RBV	Questionnaire survey/correlation analysis

Theme	Author(s)	Focus of study / contribution	Unit of analysis	Theoretical perspective	Applied methodology
	Nellore and Soderquist (2000)	Combines purchasing portfolio idea with product specifications to identify most appropriate suppliers	Buyer firm	Contingency theory	Case studies
	Petroni and Panciroli (2002)	Buyer assigns different roles to supplier in product development depending on innovative capabilities	Supplier firm	RBV	Questionnaire survey/Structural equation modelling
	Vonderembse et al. (2006)	Identify different supply chain strategies based on product characteristics and stages of product life cycle	Network	Contingency theory	Case studies
	Wynstra and Pierick (2000)	Introduces supplier involvement portfolio to distinguish degrees of supplier involvement in development projects	Buyer firm	Contingency theory	Case study
Managing inter-organisational relationships (supplier development, management, trust, sustainability, etc.)	Ballou et al. (2000)	Recognises that the management of inter-firm relationships requires intra-functional, inter-functional and inter-organisational coordination	Buyer firm	SCM	Conceptual
	Croom (2001)	In managing interactions with suppliers, relational capabilities have a significant impact on collaborative product development performance	Buyer firm	RBV	Interviews / Observation
	Harland and Knight (2001)	Identify specific roles for network management	Buyer firm	SCM	Action research/Case study
	Koufteros et al. (2005)	Internal integration is an important enabler of external integration with a supplier or a customer	Buyer firm	Contingency theory	Questionnaire survey/Structural equation modelling

Table 4. (Continued).

Theme	Author(s)	Focus of study / contribution	Unit of analysis	Theoretical perspective	Applied methodology
	Lakemond et al. (2006)	Discusses various forms of supplier involvement in product development and the managerial implications related to their coordination	Buyer firm	Contingency theory	Case studies
	Möller and Svahn (2003)	Proposes a classification of different types of relationships and the different types of capabilities needed to manage these	Network	Industrial network theory, DCV	Conceptual
	Petersen et al. (2005)	Investigates managerial practices important to effectiveness in new product development through the involvement of suppliers	Dyad	New product development, Strategic sourcing	Questionnaire survey/Structural equation modelling
	Ritter (1999)	Introduce the concept of network competence, a company specific capability to build and use inter-organisational relationships	Buyer firm	RBV	Standardised interviews/Regression analysis
	Wagner and Hoegl (2006)	Supplier involvement needs not only to be managed on the organisational but more importantly on the project level	Buyer firm	Relational view	Case study/Interviews
Impacts / benefits of inter-organisational relationships (competitive advantage, risk sharing, learning, etc.)	Carter (2005)	Shows that purchasing acting socially responsible (purchasing social responsibility) improves supplier performance and thereby reduces cost	Buyer firm	RBV, Organisational learning	Questionnaire survey/Structural equation modelling

Theme	Author(s)	Focus of study / contribution	Unit of analysis	Theoretical perspective	Applied methodology
	Dyer and Singh (1998)	Argue for the relationship as source for competitive advantage based on relations assets, knowledge sharing routines, complementary resources and effective governance	Dyad	Relational view	Conceptual
	Janda et al. (2002)	A relational orientation is positively related to product quality but negatively to acquisition cost	Buyer firm	TCE	Questionnaire survey/Structural equation modelling
	Martínez Sánchez and Pérez Pérez (2003)	Cooperation increases the ability to reduce time and cost of new product development through the use of related NPD practices	Supplier firm	Contingency approach	Questionnaire survey/Regression analysis
	Petersen et al. (2005)	Supplier involvement in product development facilitates better decision making and leads to better design quality	Dyad	New product development, Strategic sourcing	Questionnaire survey/Structural equation modelling
	Primo and Amundson (2002)	Impact of supplier involvement on product quality, project development and project cost	Buyer firm	Contingency Theory	Survey/Structural equation modelling
	Van der Valk and Wynstra (2005)	Benchmarking study reveals that supplier involvement in product development can have positive effects on performance but largely depends on the management of the relationship	Buyer firm	SCM, Strategic sourcing	Case studies
Inter-organisational relationships in automotive industry	Cusumano and Takeishi (1991)	Shows that Japanese suppliers perform better in dimensions such as quality and price compared to U.S. suppliers	Buyer firm	Relational view	Questionnaire survey/Interviews/Correlation analysis

Table 4. (Continued).

Theme	Author(s)	Focus of study / contribution	Unit of analysis	Theoretical perspective	Applied methodology
	Dyer (1997)	Reveals that high asset specificity and low transaction cost can be achieved simultaneously based on effective inter-organisational relationships	Buyer firm	TCE	Interviews
	Dyer and Hatch (2004)	Argues that sharing knowledge in close partnerships can be a source of competitive advantage	Buyer firm	Organisational learning, Knowledge based view	Case study of Toyota
	Garel and Midler (2001)	Demonstrates that co-development in relationships plays a major role in reducing the number and cost of modifications in the development process	Buyer firm	Concurrent engineering, Strategic sourcing	Case studies
	Geffen and Rothenberg (2000)	Strong partnerships are a significant element of the successful development of innovation	Buyer firm	Strategic sourcing, Relational view	Case studies

Table 5. Classification of literature on inter-organisational relationship governance

Unit of analysis		Theoretical perspectives		Applied methodology	
Individual firm[6]	10	Resource based view (RBV)	30	Case study	46
Buyer firm	92	Dynamic capabilities view (DCV)	4	Questionnaire survey	49
Supplier firm	9	Knowledge based view (KBV)	9	Longitudinal study	4
Dyad	39	Competence theory	4	Conceptual	44
Network	10	Transaction cost economics (TCE)	24	Action research	2
		Contingency theory	24	Interview	27
		Relational view	30	Observation	1
		Interaction model	5	Secondary data	11
		Complexity theory	1	Correlation analysis	23
		Strategic sourcing	23	Regression analysis	17
		Supply chain management (SCM)	12	Factor analysis	3
		Organisational learning	7	Structural Equation Modelling	18
		Portfolio modelling	4		
		Resource dependency theory (RDT)	15		
		Not identified	7		
Total	160		199[7]		245[8]

---

[6] Not specified as buyer or supplier
[7] Multiple entries were possible
[8] Multiple entries were possible

However, rather than developing a concise framework they produce guidelines on how to manage product development processes in what they call 'networked enterprises' based on empirical insights gained from six cases. Vonderembse *et al.* (2006) apply case study research to develop a framework for categorising and selecting different supply chain types according to certain product characteristics and the stages of the product life cycle. Finally, Johnsen *et al.* (2000) use findings from two extensive case studies to identify nine important networking activities related to the process of establishing and operating supply networks. Drawing on the relational view they argue that these activities are mutually supportive in that they are concerned with the tying of resources and bonding of actors.

Similarly, researchers such as Amit and Schoemaker (1993) and De Toni and Tonchia (2003) argue that traditional 'outside-in' (exogenous) and 'inside-out' (endogenous) views of the firm need to be integrated, complemented and balanced as excessive focus on either approach is not beneficial. For example, on the one hand, governance choices may have a significant impact on how rents created through valuable resources are appropriated (Barney *et al.*, 2001); and on the other hand, capability differences can be seen as a necessary condition for vertical specialisation (Jacobides and Winter, 2005). However, to date a simple conceptual framework addressing this in the context of inter-firm relationship governance is currently absent from the literature (Fynes *et al.*, 2005; Narasimhan and Nair, 2005). Borys and Jemison (1989) even went as far as calling inter-organisational governance forms 'theoretical orphans' as they have not been sufficiently addressed.

4.2. A POLYVALENT BODY OF KNOWLEDGE

Many researchers (e.g. Croom *et al.*, 2000; Ho *et al.*, 2002; Ilinitch *et al.*, 1996; Ketchen and Giunipero, 2004; Min and Mentzer, 2000; Svensson, 2003; Trienekens and Beulens, 2001) argue that a cross-fertilisation of theories from related fields is necessary for a further theoretical development and conceptual grounding of supplier management. Based on our literature review described above, we identified the following disciplines and research areas that provide relevant insights into sustainable supplier management by the means of collaborative inter-organisational relationship governance:

- **Organisational Economics** - Inter-firm relationships are social economic ties which results in responsibility and relationships
- **Strategic Management** – mainly concerned with the strategic positioning of a company in its environment to gain competitive advantage and hence could explain the competitiveness of inter-firm relationships in its industrial context as well as the positioning of partners within the relationship
- **Organisation Science** - sees organisations as ever changing phenomena based on the market circumstances they exist in (population ecology). The original work on organisation design and behaviour addressed the design of mechanisms for integrating activities across units within firms. More recent work has extended this view to include mechanisms for integrating activities across organisations
- **Industrial Marketing Management** - the voluntary exchange process of value between parties, internal and external to the boundaries of a firm, to create customer satisfaction (Kotler, 1997)
- **Purchasing and Supply Chain Management** - as it is understood today, this remains a fragmented amalgam of knowledge rooted in various antecedent theoretical concepts such as production economics, industrial dynamics, transportation and inventory decisions, social theory, marketing and purchasing (Cooper *et al.*, 1997a; Croom *et al.*, 2000; Mabert and Venkataramanan, 1998). Hence, despite strong attention on the topic over the past few years by scholars and practitioners alike (Cooper *et al.*, 1997b) there is no unified conceptual understanding of supply chains and their management; which not only leads to a great deal of differing definitions (cf. Croom *et al.*, 2000; Mentzer *et al.*, 2001) but also limits the applicability of the concept in practice (Chen and Paulraj, 2004; Mentzer *et al.*, 2001). However, the common value of most definitions can be seen as their focus on the coordination of activities and processes between the organisation and its external environment in order to create customer value (Cooper *et al.*, 1997a).

Nevertheless, it needs to be mentioned that none of the outlined disciplines and its theoretical perspectives can sufficiently explain the sustainable governance of complex constellations of inter-organisational relationships to their full extent. Although these approaches can be seen as complementary tools for the governance of inter-organisational relationships

(Trienekens and Beulens, 2001), their aggregation and application to whole-company to whole-company relationships is far too simplistic and can even be contradictory. However, a partial integration that considers the evolution of inter-organisational relationships and the development of inter-organisational structures around the delivery of a particular product or process is feasible and desirable (Sydow, 1992). A summary of the body of knowledge, i.e. the applied disciplines, their theoretical perspectives, and their relevance for the sustainable governance of inter-organisational R&D relationships, is shown in Table 6.

Similar discussions drawing on different theoretical perspectives in the context of inter-organisational relationships can be found in Ellegaard *et al.* (2003) who provide a synopsis of TCE, relationship marketing and Industrial Marketing and Purchasing (IMP). Olsen and Ellram (1997a) compare the basic concepts of marketing, purchasing and IMP, whereas Trienekens and Beulens (2001) provide an overview of perspectives within SCM, Strategic Management, Organisational Economics emphasising their complementarity in the context of inter-organisational relationships. Gulati *et al.* (2000) consider strategic networks in the context of TCE, RBV and IO issues, in a similar fashion to Dyer and Singh (1998) who compare IO, RBV and the Relational View of the firm. Sydow (1992), and Grandori and Soda (1995) provide the most comprehensive overviews drawing on a plethora of economic, political and inter-organisational theories.

Table 6. Polyvalent body of knowledge related to inter-organisational relationship governance

Discipline	Theoretical perspective	Key issues	Relevance for inter-firm relationship governance
Organisational Economics	Transaction Cost Economics	Search for most economic mechanism to govern transaction Efficacy of mechanism determined by transactions specificity, uncertainty and frequency Contracts safeguard bounded rationality and opportunism Ignores necessity to collaborate even if not transaction cost economic	Identification of appropriate inter-organisational forms to govern collaborative transactions in inter-firm relationships
Strategic Management	Industrial Organisation Theory	Competitive advantage determined by external industry factors Sees inter-firm relationship as means for firms to gain competitive advantage Ignores relationship as unit of competitive analysis	Positioning and role of individual partners within inter-firm relationship based on competencies relevant to joint R&D and product development in order to gain competitive advantage for whole relationships and partners within competitive empirical context
	Competence Theory	Competitive advantage determined by internal resource base Resources are heterogeneous and imperfectly mobile Firms should be considered as portfolios of competencies Ignore external context and rigidities that can be caused by competencies	
	Resource Dependency Theory	Firms are interdependent due to restricted availability of resources Control over critical resources determines power position relative to other firm Collaboration reduces autonomy but enables access to resources	

Table 6. (Continued).

Discipline	Theoretical perspective	Key issues	Relevance for inter-firm relationship governance
	Value Chain Concept	Firm conceptualised as set of strategically relevant activities Focus on value creation rather than cost Conceptualisation of joint product development process as virtual value chain	
Organisation Science	Contingency Theory	Organisational structure dependent on fit with internal and external contingencies as well as strategic choice of decision maker Inter-firm relationship require twofold fit Lacks of explanations for re-configuration of structures as contingencies change	(Re)structuring of inter-organisational relationships to be adaptive to environmental (exogenous) and internal (endogenous) contingencies
	Complex Adaptive Systems	Organisations are complex adaptive systems that co-evolve within social ecosystem Trade-off between internal structural consistency and fit to external contingencies needs to be managed Change occurs radically rather than moderately	
Industrial Marketing Management	Relational View	Boundary-less organisation through elimination of boundaries within and across firm boundaries Close relations create joint customer value in form of relational rents	Establishing close relationships within and across company boundaries to create customer value
	Interaction model of Industrial Marketing and Purchasing (IMP) Group	Relationship as most important resource for a firm Interaction options of actors depend on their position in network	

Discipline	Theoretical perspective	Key issues	Relevance for inter-firm relationship governance
Purchasing & Supply Chain Management	Total System Optimisation	Views supply chain as single entity tying individual success to success of overall supply system	Building and managing effective inter-organisational relationship based on total system optimisation and strategic sourcing
	Strategic Sourcing	Move from traditional commodity purchasing to business relationship management Total cost of relationship becomes crucial	

4.3. SUMMARY

This Chapter has presented the topic of inter-organisational relationships and their governance and embedded it in an interdisciplinary body of knowledge outlining the most relevant theoretical perspectives and their contribution. Thereby, the relevant literature on inter-organisational relationships was reviewed from a selected list of 40 relevant journals. The review revealed that there are gaps to be found in various dimensions of research, such as the

- Necessity to create a synthesised (i.e. holistic and integrated) model of inter-organisational relationships by not focusing on individual firms but embedding dyadic relationships in their network context
- Necessity for taking a multi-perspective approach by addressing multiple theoretical issues related to inter-organisational relationship governance
- Necessity for more qualitative theory-building research on inter-organisational relationship governance that proposes normative rather than descriptive models
- Necessity of investigating the process of establishing and developing inter-organisational relationships, especially at early stages of collaboration
- Necessity to explore dynamic aspects of inter-organisational relationships, i.e. adaptation and reconfiguration of roles and governance structures
- Necessity to establish models that enable to optimise performance and thereby sustain inter-organisational relationships

These insights provide the theoretical grounding and point of departure for this research which is described in Chapter 5.

AN EMPIRICAL STUDY ON INTER-ORGANISATIONAL R&D COLLABORATION IN THE CAR INDUSTRY

"If a qualitative study is rigorously done, I suspect that it is more likely to yield important discoveries than a quantitative study, if for no other reason than this: qualitative researchers often discover something because they usually approach topics with little clue as to what they'll find" (Barley, 2006; p. 19).

Investigating the automotive industry is not only topical due to its current challenges and problems based on the economic crisis but also because it is still one of the most important industries in the world. It is now commonly believed that the competitive performance of whole networks or supply chains rather than single firms is central to modern supply chain management (Christopher, 1998; Gomes-Casseres, 1994) and that partnerships using the most efficient and effective structure and processes will ultimately dominate their chosen markets.

5.1. RESEARCH OBJECTIVES

Therefore the central question for this empirical study was to investigate:

How can inter-firm relationships be made beneficial for each company in a supply network as well as for the collaborative network as a whole?

More specifically, the research objectives were to:

- Explore the current practice of collaboration within inter-organisational relationships in the German automotive industry
- Determine strategic factors and contingencies that influence the creation and management of inter-organisational relationships and the development and management of related inter-organisational governance structures
- Determine operative practices and tools that influence transactions and collaborative activities within inter-organisational relationships
- Develop guidelines for achieving sustainable competitive success of inter-organisational relationships.

5.2. POINT OF DEPARTURE

The methodological point of departure for the empirical work is a lack of testable theoretical propositions and hypotheses, which makes the approach of hypothesis testing inappropriate. This is because not enough explicit hypotheses exist or are too abstract to be tested in a large scale deductive manner due to the embryonic stage of hypothesis-generating research on strategic supply management issues (Handfield and Melnyk, 1998). Furthermore, investigating and analysing the governance aspects of inter-organisational relationships requires attention to details of contextually rich data and the understanding of subjective experience of employees which cannot be reflected in quantifiable variables of quantitative hypothesis-testing research (Auerbach and Silverstein, 2003).

Such research is rather exploratory in nature which favours an empirical and more qualitative hypothesis-generating research approach rather than theory testing (Eisenhardt, 1989; Snow and Thomas, 1994). This will provide the necessary openness and flexibility to gain a sound understanding of the research topic by grasping the 'hows' and 'whys' of it and thereby uncovering themes not previously accounted for in the existing literature (Leary, 2001), for instance, a "strategy concerned with the discovery of substantive theory, not with feeding quantitative researchers" is necessary (Glaser and Strauss, 1971; p. 289).

Since this research aims at extending current theory on sustainable supplier management through hypotheses generation and theory building,

Grounded Theory Method (Glaser and Strauss, 1967) was chosen as an inductive qualitative theory building approach.

5.3. GROUNDED THEORY METHOD

Grounded Theory Method (GTM) offers a "compromise between extreme empiricism and complete relativism" (p. 634) by articulating a middle ground in which systematic data collection is used to develop theories that address the interpretive realities of actors in social settings (Suddaby, 2006).

It is particularly appropriate when:

(i)   research and theory are at their early, formative stage and not enough is known on the phenomenon to state hypotheses prior to the investigation

(ii)   the major research interest lies in the identification and categorisation of elements and the exploration of their connections within social settings (Auerbach and Silverstein, 2003).

GTM research uses the basic principles of (1) questioning rather than measuring and (2) generating hypotheses using coding techniques (Auerbach and Silverstein, 2003). It enables the researcher to 'ground' the hypotheses in the empirical data: "Most hypotheses and concepts not only come from the data, but are systematically worked out in relation to the data during the course of the research" (Glaser and Strauss, 1967; p. 6). Hence, this method is an 'envelope' with the unique ability to cultivate fruitful insights from a great variety of sources and evidence - documents, archival records, artefacts, interviews, transcripts of meetings, questionnaire answers, field observations, etc. – which enables the researcher to group the holistic and meaningful characteristics of reality and therefore understand complex social phenomena (Glaser, 1978).

GTM achieves this by an iterative, process-orientated, analytic procedure using the two key operations: *constant comparison* and *theoretical sampling*. These operations are essential to develop dense, tightly woven and integrated theories and are the major difference between the grounded style and other qualitative research strategies such as case study research (Strauss, 1987). The process normally begins with the definition of a research problem, proceeds to the collection of the relevant data and continues onto a tentative explanation of that problem via forming provisional categories and abstractions of the data (involving constant comparison). This comparison challenges the properties of the initial concepts and categories and the researcher needs to go back to redefinition of the propositions and/or to further data collection and analysis (theoretical sampling). The researcher moves back and forth between data collection, coding and interpretation in an iterative manner (analytic induction) until theoretical saturation is achieved (when newly analysed data do not prompt further changes to the concepts) which leads to a tightly woven theory that emerges from and is 'grounded' in the data when, "They [the collection, codification and interpretation] should blur and intertwine continually, from the beginning of an investigation to its end" (Glaser and Strauss, 1967; p. 43).

In the following section we give an empirical example of how GTM was applied to a research study on the governance of inter-organisational supply relationships based in the German automotive industry that has resulted in the development of a novel framework grounded in empirical data.

5.4. RESEARCH APPROACH

In order to facilitate the elements of constant comparison and theoretical sampling sufficiently, ultimately leading to theoretically saturated propositions, and eventually a novel concept, the methodological research process of this particular study was structured in four main phases as shown in Figure 8 design, data collection, data coding and analysis, and data validation. A similar approach and research design has been adopted by other scholars in comparable research studies (e.g. Baines *et al.*, 1999).

Design Phase

For this research we used a combination of convenience and snowball sampling by recruiting interview participants with whom we had access to through personal contacts and asking those participants to provide further contacts. In Grounded Theory research the sample size cannot be determined in advance because each research participant potentially embodies the opportunity to develop and refine theory (Auerbach and Silverstein, 2003). In alignment with Eisenhardt's (1991) and Stake's (1995) opinion, the researcher has to keep recruiting and interviewing research participants until no new data is produced that adds new insights to theory construction or no new information is learned about the research topic. This procedure is called 'theoretical sampling' (Glaser and Strauss, 1967) and ultimately determines the sample size of the study (Auerbach and Silverstein, 2003). This approach was followed throughout the interview phase of this study which involved iterative steps in data collection and analysis in order to determine a certain level of saturation ('overlapping data analysis'; Eisenhardt, 1989). For instance, subsequent interviews became informed by analytic questions and hypotheses about data relationships drawn from previous interviews (Strauss, 1987).

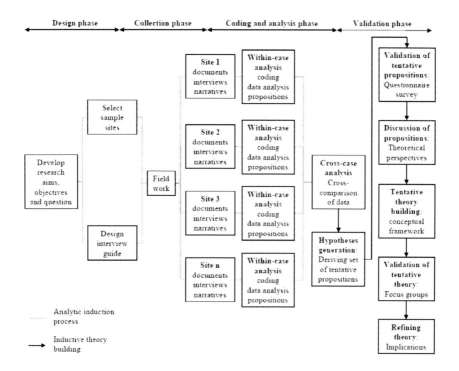

Figure 8. Outline of research approach (Adapted from Yin, 2003).

Data Collection Phase

The second stage comprised the basic data collection for this research study via interviews with experienced managers in the German automotive industry. This involved managers within car manufacturers and their suppliers who have strategic insights and responsibilities in inter-organisational collaboration; for instance those in R&D, Purchasing, Quality and Marketing/Sales (Kumar et al., 1993). A series of semi-structured interviews with a sample of 31 of these managers covering 16 companies, i.e. 4 car manufacturers and 12 supplier firms, was conducted between Dec 2004 and March 2005. A demographic overview of the interview sample is given in Table 7.

Since time and resource was a constraint, we followed the recommendations of Pettigrew (1990) and Eisenhardt (1989) to select cases that would reflect extreme situations or 'polar types' to be observed. Interviews were therefore conducted in companies that reflect different roles in the supply network such as: car manufacturers, system suppliers, module suppliers, parts or components suppliers, and engineering service providers (as demonstrated by Table 7).

The interviews were designed to explore the debate in the literature. Together with the recommendation to conduct 'narrative interviews' (Auerbach and Silverstein, 2003), i.e. asking questions that take the participants through their history with the investigated phenomenon, we developed an interview guide that contained aspects on (i) the company's industrial and competitive environment, (ii) the company's value system and competence context, and (iii) the basic collaboration issues between car manufacturers and suppliers in their inter-organisational relationships.

This semi-structured interview guide was used to make comparisons between the interviews easier and reduce the possibility of influencing the interviewees (Bryman, 2004). The interview guide is given in Appendix A. The interviews were conducted face-to-face (each lasted between 1 – 2.5hrs), taped and transcribed. Each transcript, together with a summary of the initial aggregated results, was validated by the respective interviewee to ensure that the raw data was valid and reliable before any further analysis was performed (McCutcheon and Meredith, 1993). This resulted in improvements and further additions to the data. The sample proved to be large enough for achieving theoretical saturation of the gathered data.

Table 7. Demographic overview of the interview sample

Company role	Company identifier	Size		Position of interviewee	Mgt. Level
		Number of employees	Turnover € millions		
Car manufacturer (OEM)	1	50,000	25,000	General Manager Design Car Body	Senior
				General Manager Central Quality Assurance	Senior
				General Manager Purchasing Electronics	Senior
	2	100,000	47,000	General Manager Design Doors	Middle
				Project Manager Purchasing	Junior
				Head of Concept Development Project X	Junior
	3	340,000	89,000	General Manager Design Car Body	Senior
	4	2,500	-	Head of Department Body and Trim	Senior
Systems supplier (Tier 1 and 2)	5	75,000	10,000	Sales Director	Senior
				R&D Director	Senior
	6	6,000	1,400	Sales Manager	Middle
				R&D Manager	Middle
	7	18,000	2,500	Managing Director R&D	Senior
	8	6,000	980	General Manager Customer Team	Senior
				General Manager Integration and Logistics	Senior
	9	50,000	9,600	Vice President Regional Account Executive	Senior
				Corporate Vice President Logistics	Senior

Table 7. (Continued).

Company role	Company identifier	Size		Position of interviewee	Mgt. Level
		Number of employees	Turnover € millions		
Module supplier (Tier 1 and 2)	10	450	110	General Manager Pneumatics	Senior
				General Manager Mechatronic Drives	Senior
				Manager Electronics Development	Middle
				Chief Engineering Mechatronic Drives	Junior
	11	400	40	Sales Manager	Junior
				R&D Director	Senior
	12	2,500	240	General Manager Sales and Marketing	Middle
				Deputy General Manager Customer Team 3	Middle
	13	1,300	180	Managing Director R&D	Senior
				General Manager Pisteon Rods	Middle
Parts / component supplier (Tier 2)	14	200	50	General Manager Logistics	Senior
				Managing Director	Top / Executive
Engineering service provider (Tier 1 and 2)	15	900	100	Project Manager	Junior
	16	3,000	220	Managing Branch Director	Top / Executive

Data Codification and Analysis Phase

The textual analysis of the transcribed pages of data via codification was done using the QSR NVIVO 2.0^{TM} software tool based on the constant comparative method of GTM (Glaser and Strauss, 1967). Strauss and Corbin's (1998) hierarchical coding paradigm was applied. We used open, axial and selective coding in order to reach the necessary conceptual density. It was applied at the intra and inter case level (each interview reflecting one individual case) as suggested by Strauss (1987).

Firstly, codes and categories were identified in an unrestricted open coding of the empirical data (giving 237 datum types). This gave an initial bottom-up insight into the empirical data and is a critical aspect of constant comparison required by grounded theory. Secondly, axial coding of these provisional categories gave further insight about the inter-relationships of these categories; this technique revolves around the axis of one category at a time (Strauss, 1987) (giving 158 usable codes, 16 analytical categories and 19 sub-categories).   Finally, top-down selective coding was used to develop 5 high level core categories or 'themes' that pulled together all the other detailed categories conceptually. These themes are:

(i)   industrial impact
(ii)   enterprise design
(iii)   enterprise management
(iv)   competence as contingency factor and
(v)   enterprise competitiveness.

A generic overview of the coding is given in Figure 9 showing the core categories and their related categories and sub-categories.

The findings of the codification were summarised by developing a set of 35 tentative propositions in which the conceptual framework is grounded. These parsimoniously summarise all the main issues contained in the interview transcriptions and tie the theoretical debate (summarised by the semi-structured interview guide) to industrial practice. All codes were used to form the propositions via theoretical narratives drawing on the relationships of the codes and their respective core categories. The resulting set of propositions is listed in Table 8 (see central column).

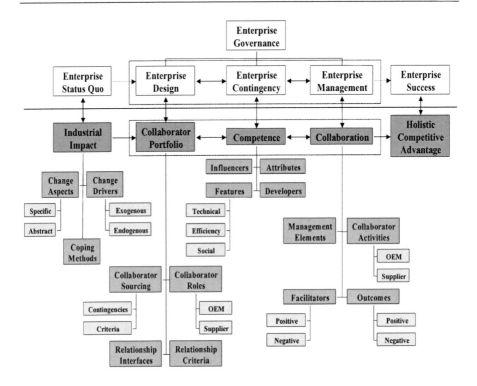

Figure 9. Generic Coding Diagram.

Data Validation Phase

To strengthen the transferability, dependability and conformity of the data (Jick, 1979), the 35 propositions were validated with a wider audience of practitioners using a questionnaire survey (see Appendix B for questionnaire). By February 2006 (a 12 weeks survey period) 110 valid responses were received from industrial experts across 52 different automotive companies, i.e. OEMs and suppliers. A breakdown of the questionnaire respondents is given in Table 9 structured by company role, functional experience and management level.

Table 8. Inducted (and validated) propositions (N=110)

Core category	No.	Proposition	Mean Agreement	Mean Importance
Relationship Status Quo (Industrial Impact)	# 1	Change in the automotive industry is driven by a combination of general industrial forces and internal company issues	1.24	4.01
	# 2	Increasing complexity, cost pressure and shorter product development lead times have led to more inter-firm collaboration based on product modularisation	1.15	4.21
	# 3	Car manufacturer are changing their adversarial pricing policies in supplier selection towards more strategic sourcing policies	-0.38	4.10
	# 4	The challenge for a collaborative supply network is to maintain competitiveness without applying adversarial forces	0.70	3.94
	# 5	Focusing on core competencies is becoming increasingly important in order to drive the development and management of inter-firm collaboration in the supply network	0.90	3.82
	# 6	Structure of the supply network is determined by the strategy of the car manufacturer	0.98	3.71
	# 7	Product modularisation affects how a supply network is structured	1.18	3.94
	# 8	Different relationships and collaborative practices exist for different inter-company (car manufacturer and supplier) projects in the supply network	1.21	3.47
	# 9	The role of an organisation in the supply network is mainly determined by what competencies are offered by it	1.23	4.21
Relationship Design (Collaborator Portfolio)	# 10	The role of an organisation in the supply network is partly determined by the stages of the product development process	0.91	3.60
	# 11	Relationships between companies in the supply network change over time	1.18	3.68
	# 12	An individual company can collaborate in more than one project within the supply network at the same time	1.37	3.54
	# 13	An inter-firm collaboration in the supply network needs to be formed on the basis of technical competencies and mutual exchange of knowledge	0.87	3.76
	# 14	There is the need for a coordinator and leader within the supply network that has the competence to evaluate and manage the interfaces in a collaboration	1.30	4.13
	# 15	The co-ordinator of the supply network should have its own core competencies and encourage those of other organisations to participate	1.37	4.08

No.	Proposition	Mean Agreement	Mean Importance
# 16	Competencies of separate organisations participating in a collaboration within the supply network need to be linked via cross-company project infrastructures	0.80	3.75
# 17	Different projects in the supply network have to be managed differently	1.00	3.62
# 18	Overly stable relationships between companies in the supply network can lead to a loss of innovativeness	-0.31	3.31
# 19	New inter-firm collaborations produce innovative solutions	0.84	3.77
# 20	Car manufacturers still retain overall responsibility for the management of the whole supply network	0.30	3.76
# 21	To become more influential in the supply network a company must take responsibility for integrating other companies and their products	0.90	3.70
# 22	Early and intense integration of strategic collaborators facilitates the successful delivery of a project within the supply network	1.64	4.28
# 23	At early stages of the collaboration process technical and social rather than monetary aspects have to be measured and compared	1.06	4.13
# 24	Strategic and long term thinking for the whole supply network increases the chance of successful inter-firm collaboration	1.42	4.19
# 25	The boundaries of responsibilities between collaborating parties need to be clearly defined to deliver a successful inter-firm project within the supply network	1.69	4.51
# 26	Functional and short-term thinking within an organisation produces sub-optimisation for the supply network	0.96	3.71
# 27	The existence of cross-functional units that can act autonomously from other parts of the same company facilitate inter-firm collaboration	0.30	3.55
# 28	To operate autonomously within the organisation and to integrate in the supply network cross-functional units must have both unique resources and interface capabilities	0.82	3.55
# 29	The more mature, attractive and transferable a competence is the more potential value it can create for the supply network	1.17	3.90
# 30	Competencies can be developed and deployed through collaboration with other companies in the supply network	1.06	3.73

Relationship Management (Collaboration): # 21 – # 27

Relationship Contingency (Competence): # 28 – # 30

Table 8. (Continued).

Core category	No.	Proposition	Mean Agreement	Mean Importance
	# 31	For each new inter-firm project a new appropriate supply base has to be selected and managed	0.20	3.64
Relationship Success (Holistic Competitive Advantage)	# 32	There is a positive correlation between the extent of inter-firm collaboration and the sustainable success of the supply network and its individual companies	0.62	3.50
	# 33	Establishing inter-firm collaboration is an effective way of improving quality and innovation of products as well as reducing development lead-times and cost in a supply network	1.05	4.04
	# 34	The short term success of inter-firm collaboration in the supply network is related to cost and lead time reduction	1.09	4.01
	# 35	The long term success of inter-firm collaboration in the supply network is related to quality and innovation improvement	0.93	4.10

Table 9. Overview of the validation questionnaire respondents

Company role	No. of responses	Functional experience	No. of responses	Management level	No. of Responses
Car manufacturer	38	R&D / Styling	75	Clerk	18
Systems supplier	52	Purchasing	15	Junior Management	27
Module supplier	33	Quality assurance	13	Middle Management	35
Parts / component supplier	30	Production / manufacturing	15	Senior Management	22
Assembly service provider	4	Logistics	7	Top Management	3
Logistics service provider	2	Marketing / Sales	36	Other	5
Engineering service provider	27	Strategy / directorship	25		
Other	9	Other	13		
	Σ = 195		Σ = 199		Σ = 110

This stage established whether respondents agreed with the researchers' analysis and interpretation of the raw interview data on inter-organisational relationships and whether they thought the observations were important enough to warrant building into a consolidated novel concept. The respondents ranked their perceptions on the two dimensions 'Agreement' and 'Importance' in interval levels using a 5-point Likert scale as follows:

- *Agreement* (strongly agree =2, agree =1, neutral = 0, disagree = -1, strongly disagree = -2); Positive scores indicate agreement and negative scores indicate disagreement.
- *Importance* (very high = 5, high = 4, medium = 3, low = 2, very low = 1); All positive scores were used as this was a weighting factor.

The results of this exercise are included in Table 8 above. The evaluation of the propositions through a survey of industrial experts provided feedback on the quality and adequacy of the data coding and analysis which enabled further conceptual development and inductive theory building (Glaser, 1978). However, the validation of tentative propositions must *not* be confused with quantitative hypotheses testing; the purpose of grounded theory method is only to *code* data enough to be able to *generate and suggest* theory *not to prove* it statistically (Glaser, 1994). The detailed methodology used is described further in Binder and Edwards (2010).

5.5. NOVEL EMPIRICAL FINDINGS

The empirical research showed that inter-organisational collaboration is generally regarded as an effective means to maintain and achieve competitiveness for the whole supply network and its individual member companies with short-term (e.g. cost and lead time reduction) and long-term effects (e.g. quality and innovation improvement). Each member of the supply network and the supply network as a whole is thereby challenged by a variety of exogenous and endogenous forces, such as increasing product complexity, shorter development lead times, increasing cost pressure etc., leading to increased collaboration activities that are increasingly carried out on a modular basis rather than a parts or component basis.

In this context, strategic sourcing based on proactive supplier management and a focus on competencies and collaborative partnerships are considered principle factors for the development and management of successful supply networks and relationships therein. This is because competencies together with the stages of the product development process are the main determinant of the role of the individual partners in the collaborative venture via the value they are creating for the supply network. Therefore, companies should possess 'unique sales propositions' (e.g. innovativeness, R&D knowledge, etc.) which enables the differentiation from competitors; but they should also have interface capabilities that enable the linking with partners in the supply network (e.g. project management, organisational structure, etc.). This is necessary because individual companies collaborating within a supply network have to be linked via cross-company projects for the effective and efficient development and deployment of their competencies.

Research results showed that at the early stages of R&D collaboration within a supply network, competence development and transfer (technical and knowledge based exchanges) rather than transactional cost optimisation should be the primary focus for sourcing and collaboration activities. This may be because competence development and the exchange of related knowledge are seen as important precursors to establishing effective operational R&D transactions. In the opinion of the industrial experts, this is best achieved by taking a long term strategic view, an intense integration of partners at early stages of a project and the creation of autonomous cross-functional units within the collaborating partner companies. This is preferable to taking a sub-optimal view based upon organisational functions, departments or business units that are focused on individual partner companies rather than the whole supply network.

Furthermore, the existence of a multiplicity of dynamic relationships and projects within a supply network require differentiated management based on the respective project and relationship characteristics. It also requires a leader or coordinator who has enough competencies to clearly define boundaries of responsibility within an inter-organisational R&D project and manage the resulting interfaces between the collaborating partners. In order to pursue this coordination and interface successfully, the coordinator needs to own sufficient competencies themselves, but also be able to encourage the participating partners to contribute their own know-how allowing for a certain degree of autonomy within the collaborative venture. This is true for the whole car as well as individual sub-systems and modules. This implies that becoming more influential within the supply network also requires managing competencies and products belonging to other collaborating companies.

In this context, the validation showed that the strategic design of the supply network via the selection and sourcing of appropriate partners remains the responsibility of the car manufacturer. The supply network is also influenced by product modularisation which is also driven by the car manufacturer. However, the operational management may be executed by other significant partners within the network such as the prime contractors or the first tier system suppliers (cf. Figure 2 above). Either way, although new inter-company constellations can be a stimulus for innovation, overly stable relationships between collaborating companies in the network do not automatically lead to a loss of innovativeness which can make the selection of a new supply base for each new project obsolete.

It was observed that despite all agreement on the facilitators for effective inter-organisational R&D collaboration, the validation showed that current practice in the German automotive industry *does not* apply the necessary mechanisms for good practice. This is probably due to adversarial sourcing and supplier management strategies still dominating over and above long-term orientated collaborative partnerships. However, because such a strategic partnership orientated approach towards supplier management and inter-organisational collaboration abandons price competition, a major challenge for a collaborative supply network is to maintain competitiveness without actually applying adversarial forces. Decision makers who face the challenges in governing inter-organisational relationships still need to be provided with further practical guidance in form of strategies and operational mechanisms on how to build and manage sustainable inter-organisational relationships that contain the most suitable partners.

The insights gained through this empirical research led to the development of a novel conceptual framework for sustainable supplier management, known as *Collaborative Enterprise Governance,* to facilitate managers in the automotive industry in their strategic decision making on inter-organisational relationships (see the following Chapter 6). The conceptual framework was initially validated with experts from the German automotive industry in a workshop; particularly the main elements of the novel concept, its step-by-step application and its applicability and usefulness for creating sustainable competitive advantage. Since then it has been validated through a separate study based in the UK automotive industry.

5.6. SUMMARY

The major aim of this research is to shed light upon the question:

How can inter-organisational relationships be made beneficial for each company in a supply network as well as for the collaborative network as a whole?

In this context, GTM was identified as a suitable research method that facilitates the analytic nature (what, why and how questions) of the study by extending the current literature via hypothesis-generation.

The related empirical research process of this study involved four main phases: design, data collection, data coding and analysis, and data validation. During the *design phase* research objectives were specified, data collection techniques and sample sites selected, and an interview guide for the semi-structured interviews constructed. *Data collection* in the field was deployed through a set of 28 semi-structured interviews with managers in the German automotive industry. Convenience and snowball sampling techniques were used to gain a sample of 31 participants who were taken through their experience with the investigated research topic using 'narrative interviews'. *Data coding and analysis* was performed through applying the key operations of GTM (constant comparison and theoretical sampling). In this, a hierarchy of coding levels (open, axial and selective) was used to reach the stage of hypotheses generation and theory building. During the first stage of *data validation* the developed tentative propositions were validated via a questionnaire survey (110 valid responses) assessing their importance for the studied research topic. In the second stage of *data validation* this framework has been discussed with practitioners of the German automotive industry in a focus group workshop to evaluate the applicability of the framework and its potential for improving the competitiveness of inter-organisational R&D relationships (cf. Chapter 7 later). Further independent studies in the UK automotive industry have also been conducted recently.

Chapter 6

A CONCEPTUAL FRAMEWORK FOR SUSTAINABLE SUPPLIER MANAGEMENT

"Relationships are one of the most valuable resources that a company possesses" (Hakansson, 1987; p. 10).

In this book collaborative inter-organisational relationships are referred to as *enterprises* and the design (*enterprise design*) and management (*enterprise management*) of them as the concept of *Collaborative Enterprise Governance*. The European Commission (2003) defines an *enterprise* as "… an entity, regardless of its legal form … including partnerships or associations regularly engaged in economic activities". Therefore, in its most simple form an *enterprise* could be a single integrated company. However, this concept builds on the distinctive assumption that *enterprises* can also be made up of autonomous parts of different individual companies (*enterprise modules*) because existing observations fail to emphasise that the examples they cite are drawn from only *one part* of a large company, whilst other parts of the same company are operating on a completely different *modus operandi* with their own partners and suppliers.

To explain this behaviour this concept uses the term *enterprise* (to emphasise joint collaboration) and its sub-units known as *enterprise modules* (to allow part-to-part company relationships to be explored) as unit of analyses thereby embedding single dyadic relationships between collaborating partners (e.g. OEM and supplier) in their overall network context, which is characteristic of R&D projects.

6.1. THE ENTERPRISE MODULE

Similarly to the assumption made by Competence Theory, that a firm should be considered as a portfolio of competencies, the conceptual framework proposed here conceptualises an individual company as a set of autonomous entities, termed *enterprise modules*, that deliver specific competencies (e.g. special design and engineering know how) to *collaborative activities* (e.g. R&D projects) within the overall *enterprise*. Thereby, the *enterprise modules* possess all relevant competencies to perform a certain task in the project (encapsulation; Baldwin and Clark, 2006a). This forms a unique and valued proposition for the company via its *enterprise modules* drawing on aspects of competence and Resource Dependency Theory. However, these highly task specific assets need to be supported by relationship specific resources (e.g. communication technology, co-operative contracts, and shared processes) that help to intermediate the specific competencies into a viable *value stream* within the *enterprise*. This not only facilitates the design of inter-organisational governance structures, (i.e. *enterprise structures)*, with economically acceptable transaction costs but also the development (exploration) and deployment (exploitation) of competencies through the 'absorptive capacity' (Cohen and Levinthal, 1990; March, 1991) that is linked to the relationship specific assets. This draws on ideas of TCE and Relational View such that investment in relationship specific assets can generate economic rents beneficial to all parties (Dyer and Singh, 1998). In alignment with Industrial Organisation Theory and Competence Theory these competencies are then the basis for the sustainable competitive advantage of the individual partner and the holistic *enterprise* alike. Table 10 provides an overview of the elements of an *enterprise module* derived from the empirical research.

This requires strategists to overcome traditional thinking about internal sub-units being functions and departments and think differently in a modular fashion in terms of *enterprise modules*. For a collaborative approach towards supplier management this means connecting *enterprise modules* of one supplier (parts of the supplier company) with *enterprise modules* owned by other suppliers (parts of other supplier companies) in cross-company R&D projects within the *enterprise*. For instance, *enterprise modules* may be deployed in inter-organisational concurrent engineering teams supporting the idea of a boundary-less organisation of the Relational View. This is in order to create an inter-organisational structure that can meet the demands of a rapidly changing industrial environment whilst still operating within acceptable cost limits (Binder and Clegg, 2006). Similarly, Anderson *et al.* (1994) and Bititci *et al.* (2004) propose a focal dyadic relationship between supplier business units and customer business units.

Table 10. Elements of an Enterprise Module

Task specific assets (unique competencies)	Technical	Innovativeness Product know how Product and process quality R&D evaluation Interface management Delivery quality Total process partner R&D software knowledge (e.g. CAD software)
	Efficiency	Speed Cost alignment Project management Flexibility and adaptability Knowledge accessibility
Relationship specific assets (interface capabilities)	Commercial	Negotiation based on trust and fairness (collaborative contracts) Information sharing (cost) Financial stake-holding
	IT	Online sourcing platforms IT interface management
	Project	Simultaneous engineering (intra-organizational) Inter-organizational concurrent engineering Leadership (management support) Communication Inter-personal relationships Knowledge sharing
	Organizational	Collaboration infrastructure (e.g. Key account management) Cluster creation Holistic and strategic thinking
	Social	Structure and culture Customer focus Ownership Local presence Plug & play ability Stability and reliability Pressure resistance

6.2. THE ENTERPRISE MATRIX

Drawing on the basics of the *value stream* concept, the *Enterprise Matrix* tool (see Figure 10) is used to map a particular collaborative activity (e.g. an R&D project) by considering it to be an *enterprise*. It is important to stress that the *Enterprise Matrix* is not based on the activities of a single firm, but on the delivery of a collaborative project. The *value members* of the *enterprise* are listed on the vertical axis (they are listed in order of significance from the most important at the top to the least important at the bottom). There can be any number of these *value members* which could reach into the hundreds for a complex R&D project. However the different types of *value members* should be able to be classified into approximately 7 different types (c.f. Figure 2). The value stream stages are also mapped along the horizontal axis (starting with the first stage on the left hand side and the last stage on the right hand side); again there can be any number of these but usually a whole value stream can be described at a high-level quite adequately in about 4 stages (c.f. Figure 7) (Clegg and Binder, 2004). Each of the white cells in the centre of the *Enterprise Matrix* represents the conceptual location where value is created by an *enterprise module*. By filling out the *Enterprise Matrix* one can collect data about the composition of an overall enterprise in question, begin to understand its dynamics and how it should be managed. The *Enterprise Matrix* is a data collection tool for using the concept of *Collaborative Enterprise Governance* in a practical deployment.

It should be noted that the *Enterprise Matrix* tool is used as a quick deductive short cut to the more lengthy GTM theory that was originally used to induct the whole *Collaborative Enterprise Governance* concept. As the *Collaborative Enterprise Governance* concept is now established and validated, a data collection tools such as this is sufficient to use to establish which kind of *enterprise* is present in a particular project, understand its prevailing dynamics and begin to take steps to improve its performance and management.

Alternative tools and frameworks that similarly aim to integrate relationship decision making, value chains, and competencies can be found in the literature (e.g. Fine *et al.*, 2002; McIvor, 2000). Fine *et al.* (2002) acknowledged that

"Understanding and redesigning a company's value chain begins with a map, one that identifies the organizations involved, the capabilities they bring to the value proposition, and the technological contribution each makes to the company's products and services" (p. 70).

Collaborative activity:		value stream Process start ⟶ Process end			
		Stage 1	Stage 2	...	Stage n
high involvement	Member 1	Enterprise module delivered by 'member 1' in 'stage 1' of the value stream			
↑	Member 2				
value					
members	...				
↓					
low involvement	Member n				

Figure 10. The Enterprise Matrix - A tool for coordinating collaborative activities in enterprises by linking product, process and structure.

Collaboration within inter-organisational relationships is based on transactions between heterogeneous value members (e.g. OEM and suppliers) that traditionally pursue diverse strategies but try to fulfil a common task (e.g. joint product development) by establishing a mutual modus operandi through sharing knowledge and information. However, due to the specialisation and differences in knowledge (e.g. in the context of R&D and product development) difficulties occur when sharing their know-how and competencies across occupational boundaries within collaborative activities.

In this sense, the Enterprise Matrix tool helps to optimise the whole enterprise operation (represented by the respective collaborative activity) through the allocation of the most suitable value members to process stages of the value stream based on their value proposition to the enterprise (as determined by their specific competencies). Baldwin and Clark (2006b) use the notion of a 'task and transfer network' that "defines and performs tasks, transfer tasks, and matches agents to tasks in such a way that the desired goods are obtained, and no agent has to carry out tasks that are beyond its ability" (p. 5).

Thereby, this kind of allocation bridges 'structural holes' (Obstfeld, 2005) between the value members in the enterprise through the establishment of common ground based on the enterprise modules that consist of task relevant unique competencies and relationship facilitating interface capabilities. In Becker and Zirpoli's (2003) words the Enterprise Matrix tool can be seen as an artefact that helps to integrate knowledge through providing an architecture along which the value members can place their knowledge into a problem solving value stream. It is thereby important to realise that the value stream is composed only of the parts (i.e. the enterprise modules) of the value members that actually add value (value proposition) to the collaborative activity, i.e. the parts of the supply base that are actively managed by the enterprise governor (Choi and Krause, 2006; Hines and Rich, 1997).

A collaborative activity is a joint business activity in the enterprise and can involve a product (e.g. car, or car component), a service (e.g. a financial service for car leasing), or a project (e.g. a construction project) that should be reasonably defined and circumscribed. This task should be conducted by a distinct leader, i.e. the project owner, who should have the competence to evaluate the enterprise modules of the value members, allocate suitable modules and their competencies to respective stages and tasks of the value stream, and define the responsibilities of and boundaries between the value members. This is especially crucial at the early stages of the value stream in order to deliver successful collaborative activities and needs to be applied for each new collaborative activity (e.g. R&D project) within the enterprise.

As argued elsewhere (Binder and Clegg, 2006) this competence of governing, i.e. designing and managing, collaborative enterprises can be considered as meta-competence or interface competence, i.e. a competence that affects the capability to coordinate (Liedtka, 1999), which requires an overall strategic orientation towards the whole enterprise. In alignment with elements of enterprise modules (cf. Table 10 above) it involves aspects of relationship management, technology management and knowledge management, such as coordinating & intermediating, translating & designing, decision making & allocating, scouting & integrating, leading & initiating, facilitating & enabling, developing & manufacturing, and marketing & selling.

However, the responsibilities of designing and managing enterprises do not necessarily need to be occupied by a single value member but can involve various partners. In the German automotive industry it is, for example, often the case that the OEM defines the overall product specifications and selects the suitable partners for an R&D project, i.e. acting as enterprise governor or strategic supply manager but delegates the operative management of the supply base, i.e. the coordination of the collaborative activity, to a first tier prime contractor or system supplier, i.e. a significant value member. Usually this depends on strategic choice moderated by product attributes, supplier competencies, and stage of development process. Karlsson (2003) describes this as the distinction between 'feature engineering' and 'specialised engineering'. This, however, requires the OEM to move away from his traditional role as *tertius gaudens* and move towards *tertius iungens* (Obstfeld, 2005) or primus inter pares (Binder and Clegg, 2005) whereas the first tiers need to take more responsibility for integrating and coordinating products and competencies of other value members in the enterprise. This is very much in line with the interaction model of the Industrial Marketing and Purchasing Group and aspects of Resource Dependency Theory in such that the possession of critical resources (e.g. meta-competence) determines the power position and the interaction options of a value member in the enterprise.

Hence, the proximity of inter-organisational relationships in an enterprise, described by the involvement of the value members in the collaborative activity (cf. Enterprise Matrix above), can range from a high involvement relationship with influence in negotiating ones own situation through the integration of complex systems and modules as a Tier 1 systems supplier or prime contractor to some sort of 'design & make suppliers', which will typically have less influence and become a hired competence (e.g. concept design or product realization), such as Tier 2 and 3 suppliers for specific parts and components. Thereby, the degree of involvement is not only dependent upon the value proposition of the competencies but also the stages of the value stream of the collaborative activity the enterprise module and its competencies are delivered to.

For instance, during the concept phase of product development value members that possess innovative capabilities and technological product know-how can gain more influence within the collaborative activity by contributing highly to the competitive advantage of the enterprise than other value members that only deliver competencies to the later stages of series development or production. Thereby, the Enterprise Matrix is a vehicle for linking the architecture of modular products with the structure of the enterprise (i.e. supply base) in the sense of Fine's (1998) 3-DCE concept, by effectively combining the most suitable competencies of individual value members along the value stream to deliver superior products to the marketplace.

6.3. THE DYNAMIC ENTERPRISE REFERENCE GRID

The crucial part of the Collaborative Enterprise Governance concept is to determine the appropriate relationship or governance strategy, i.e. enterprise structure, between the enterprise governor as project owner (normally the OEM) and the participating value members (normally suppliers) in the collaborative activity based on the various situational contingencies discussed above. Or as Baines and Kay (2002) phrased it: "Many sourcing practices exist and the challenge is to find the right practice, for the right product, at the right time" (p. 101). Thereby, the dyadic relationship between enterprise governor and value member and between each of the value members in turn is embedded in the overall enterprise (captured by a particular collaborative activity as shown in the Enterprise Matrix) and the prevailing type defines the type of enterprise.

The empirical evidence of this research suggests that a balance of different collaborative types of inter-organisational relationship strategies and structures exist (i.e. enterprise structures), and their related relationship roles and activities is necessary for a sustainable supplier management, in order to minimise commercial risk for short-term success whilst simultaneously encouraging innovation and quality improvements for long-term success of the enterprise. In turn this facilitates the success of each individual value member participating within the collaborative enterprise.

Based on the observations made during the study, three distinct enterprise structures for the governance of collaborative enterprises could be identified. They are termed virtual (autonomous) enterprises, extended (partner) enterprises and vertically integrated (linked) enterprises. The main characteristics of the three structures are described in Table 11 which is mainly based on empirical insights but was also informed by the discussion in the existing literature.

Table 11 should be used when deploying the *Collaborative Enterprise Governance* Concept to help determine which sort of *enterprise* they are investing and mapping. For instance, is it a *virtual (autonomous) enterprise*, an *extended (partner) enterprise*, or a *vertically integrated (linked) enterprise*?

Table 11. Enterprise structures fundamental to Collaborative Enterprise Governance

Characteristics	Virtual (Autonomous) Enterprise	Extended (Partner) Enterprise	Vertically Integrated (Linked) Enterprise
Similar terms and supply chain philosophies	Virtual enterprise, virtual corporation / organisation; agile philosophy	Extended enterprise, keiretsu, clan; hybrid philosophy	Vertically integrated enterprise; lean enterprise; lean philosophy
Foundation of relationship	Mainly based on technical competence features; Emphasis on high innovation context; Decision of allocating resources depends on competitive and comparative advantage	Mainly based on social competence features; past relationship experience important; emphasis on strategic sourcing of critical products based on synergy for the whole enterprise	Mainly based on efficiency competence features; emphasis on transaction costs (prices)
Evolution of relationship based on competencies	Newly emerging, speculative, untested, high risk, require many members to spread risk; high asset specific investments; high transaction costs	Tested to some extent, medium risk, has had some testing, understood by innovators; medium asset specific investments; medium transaction costs	Mature, well accepted, tested and widely usable; low asset specific investments; low transaction costs
Scope of relationship	Project based to quickly exploit specific opportunities across company boundaries; present a unified face to externals; partners involved in other collaborative activities simultaneously for more power and maturity	Long-term and holistic thinking in collaborative dimensions; often spans whole product life cycle across company boundaries	Standardisation of high product volumes and corporisation of structures; focus on scales of economies rather than on extension and virtualisation
Longevity of relationship	Short-term temporary alignment of operations	Medium - long-term	Foreseeable as permanent (as long as competitive)
Proximity and depth of relationship	No stability as well as dynamic and unpredictable environment; collaboration impacts operations directly and immediately (agility, flexibility and leanness); low degree of interdependence and integration	Strategic dimensions of collaboration; relationship, technology and knowledge management become critical; medium degree of interdependence and integration	Tend toward industrial dominance; emphasis on removal of legacy systems; high degree of interdependence and integration

Table 11. (Continued).

Characteristics	Virtual (Autonomous) Enterprise	Extended (Partner) Enterprise	Vertically Integrated (Linked) Enterprise
Governance of relationship	Loose and flexible environment based on innovator scouting; temporary, re-active and loose governance; right balance of control and emergence (i.e. co-opetition)	Stable and strategic environment based on integration through appropriate strategic sourcing and partner development; design and implementation of business mutual processes; strategic and pro-active governance	Unity of command and control; focused on monitoring and control through standardisation and corporatisation
Strategic role and main tasks of enterprise governor	Incubator; scouting for potential value members; initiate collaborative activities	Integrator; coordination of collaborative activities; support value members in competence development	Incumbent; in-house development of proprietary systems; Relying on power and authority
Strategic role and main tasks of value members	Innovation supplier; deploying specific competencies for innovating new technologies and solving complex R&D problems	Integrator; integrating parts to more complex systems and managing and coordinating sub-supply base based on meta-competence	Volume player; value creation through cost efficient making and delivery of parts in high quality
Collaboration points in PDP	Mainly product planning and concept design	Mainly concept design / pre-series design	Mainly series design

It has been observed in this research that *virtual (autonomous) enterprises, extended (partner) enterprises* and *vertically integrated (linked) enterprises* are not, as some would believe, governance structures resulting from completely different strategies but that they are better thought of as a continuous spectrum of the same strategy focused on inter-organisational collaboration. Thereby the *vertically integrated (linked) enterprise* is the inter-company governance form that most closely approximates the traditional vertically integrated company (a single legal entity) and could be seen as a kind of proto-institution that emerges from a high level of embeddedness and integration of the partners (cf. Lawrence *et al.*, 2002). Similarly, Lambert *et al.* (1996) proposed three kinds of partnership structures depending on their short-term (Type 1), long-term (Type 2), and long-term with no end (Type 3) character.

This research suggests that an individual part of a single company (i.e. an *enterprise module*) may be part of numerous different *enterprises* that operate quite independently. For instance, an *enterprise module* of a company (i.e. *value member*) can be engaged within more than one *collaborative activity* within different *enterprises* whilst drawing upon the same specific competence. It is therefore useful to perceive *enterprises* as consisting of a collection of semi-autonomous *modules* (i.e. autonomous parts of individual companies), where each *module* is able to contribute value to a number of co-existing *enterprises structures* simultaneously, by deploying its competencies in *collaborative activities* in an *enterprise structure*. This is similar to the 'meta-system' perspective suggested by Boardman and Clegg (2001) that considers a supply chain as an organisation in its own right where each specific configuration of it forms a separate virtual organisation.

It is already recognised that competencies need to be regarded as a strategic resource which should be managed and developed in a balanced approach so that companies are prepared for changing industrial requirements. For instance, Prahalad and Hamel (1990) proposed the idea to use a portfolio of *competencies* rather than a portfolio of *businesses*. This conceptual framework uses competencies similarly, but differs from the traditional viewpoint by considering them to be an *enterprise-wide* resource rather than just an individual company's resource. Thereby, the *enterprise governance* perspective (similar to Fine's (1998) notion of capabilities chains) discusses how *competencies* are designed and delivered to a *collaborative enterprise* in order to optimise the competitiveness of the whole system through linking product, process and structure and hence differs from a traditional *supply*

chain and *operations management perspective* that primarily concentrates on
the flow of products and services *per se* (Binder and Clegg, 2007).

Thereby, the number and type of *enterprise engagements* for any one
company is closely aligned with the value proposition of its competencies and
the capability of deploying them within *collaborative activities* in the
enterprise. This is referred to as *engage-ability* of the competence in the
enterprise with regard to the respective *collaborative activity*, i.e. the ability of
a *value member* to be involved in the *collaborative activity* due to its value
proposition. In alignment with aspects of Contingency Theory, Competence
Theory and TCE, the determination of an appropriate *enterprise structure* for
the resulting governance of the inter-company relationship between *enterprise
governor* and *value member* was identified to be dependent upon three main
competence attributes that are influenced by various exogenous (external to
relationship) and endogenous (internal to relationship) factors. In other words,
the selection of an appropriate governance mode for a specific dyadic
relationship within an *enterprise* is dependent upon various exogenous and
endogenous factors that influence the value proposition of the competence
(embedded in the *enterprise module*) to the *collaborative activity* and
ultimately to the *enterprise*. The three identified competence attributes, their
related exogenous and endogenous factors (derived from RBV and TCE to
provide an integrative perspective; Madhok and Tallman, 1998) and their
impact on the *engage-ability* of the competence (and the *enterprise module*)
are outlined in Table 12.

Table 12. Attributes influencing the engage-ability of competencies in the enterprise

Competence attribute	Exogenous and endogenous factors	Impact on engage-ability (correlation)
Transferability	Competence specificity (endo)	Negative
	Transaction frequency (endo)	Positive
Attractiveness	Marketability (market value) of competence (exo)	Positive
	Uncertainty of competence value (exo)	Negative
	Suitability of competence deployment (exo)	Positive
	Risk of competence deployment (exo)	Negative
Maturity	Advancement and sophistication of competence (endo)	Positive
	Sustainability of competence (exo)	Positive

For instance, if the specificity of a competence (an endogenous factor) is
high due to specific knowledge of one particular value member the

transferability of this know-how within the collaborative activity is **low** (negative impact) resulting in a **low** engage-ability of the competence in the collaborative activity and hence the enterprise. However, the transferability and hence engage-ability of the competence can be increased as value members get more integrated over time and transaction frequency (endogenous factor) between them increases (positive impact). Similarly, a **low** marketability of a new competence (exogenous factor) due to its untested market value will result in a **low** attractiveness and hence a **low** engage-ability (positive impact). However, this market value can for example be increased through further advancement and sophistication of the competence (or related technology) (endogenous factor) leading to a **higher** maturity (positive impact), **less** risk of deployment (negative impact) and therefore **higher** market value and engage-ability of the competence.

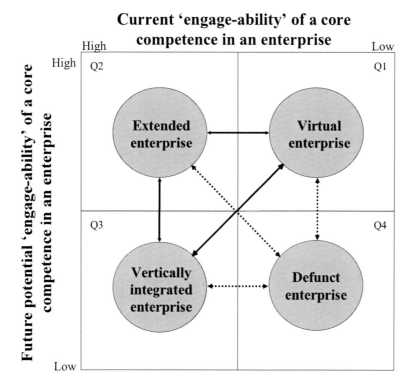

Figure 11. The Dynamic Reference Grid - determining appropriate enterprise structures.

However, these examples show that the determination of an appropriate enterprise structure for the governance of dyadic relationships in collaborative enterprises should not only be based on the current value and engage-ability of a competence (which only contributes to the current competitiveness of the enterprise and its value members) but also on its future value and engage-ability (which contributes to the future competitiveness of the enterprise and the value members).

Figure 11 summarises the findings in a concise Dynamic Enterprise Reference Grid which shows four prevailing current and future types of competencies and their engage-ability (ranked simply as 'high' or 'low'). In each of the quadrants the best suited enterprise structure (virtual, extended or vertically integrated) depending on the current and future engage-ability of the prevailing competencies is given with some of its key characteristics.

Each quadrant of the *Dynamic Enterprise Reference Grid* is now taken in turn to be characterised in more detail (also cf. Table 11 above).

Quadrant 1: Low Current Engage-Ability but High Future Potential Engage-Ability

Value members governed in this quadrant show a prevalence of competencies with low current but high future engage-ability. This is due to the possession of newly emerging competencies that are untested on the market and often are very specific to the value members. This impacts negatively on the transferability, attractiveness and maturity of these competencies and hence enterprise governor and other collaborating value members will be very reluctant to make long term plans and investments, and so arrangements will be temporary to exploit market opportunities quickly. Thereby, risks spread over many different value members to increase the chances for the generation of new knowledge. In addition, the cost of collaborating will be very high due to the fragmented resource base, high specificity of the competencies and their low ability to be integrated in the wider system of the enterprise which favours a short-term collaboration – these are characteristics of a virtual (autonomous) enterprise. In an virtual (autonomous) enterprise every value member delivers a very specific and limited value to the overall collaborative activity tailored to its very specific competence features leading to a low involvement along the value stream of a collaborative activity (cf. Enterprise Matrix above). Thereby, the selection of theses value members is mainly based on their innovative capabilities and their competence to solve complex technological problems.

Quadrant 2: High Current Engage-Ability and High Future Potential Engage-Ability

Value members governed in this quadrant possess competencies that are currently highly engaged due to matured, partly tested and market proven competencies that are also highly attractive involving low degrees of uncertainty and risk for their deployment. They are also perceived to have high potential engage-ability in the future based on high sophistication and sustainability of the competencies' value proposition. Therefore, the enterprise governor seeks more stable, strategic and medium to longer term co-developmental supply strategies with these value members to minimise commercial risks leading to more frequent transactions and competence deployments. This decreases the cost of collaboration and increases the ability to integrate these competencies closer into the enterprise – these are characteristics of an extended (partner) enterprise. In an extended (partner) enterprise the value members are more involved in the collaborative activity both in terms of proximity and longevity of the relationships often spanning the whole product life cycle. Their selection is mainly based on their interface capabilities and meta-competence that are valuable to the synergy of the enterprise often leading to the responsibility for managing other value members, i.e. integrating their competencies, on behalf of the enterprise governor.

Quadrant 3: High Current Engage-Ability but Low Future Potential Engage-Ability

Value members governed in this quadrant occupy competencies that are currently highly engaged due to their mature, well established and widely usable character. But they also have the perception of becoming less attractive in the future, e.g. due to high profits becoming eroded or technologies becoming obsolete and substituted. Therefore, the enterprise governor seeks whole ownership of the assets and capabilities which they may have become highly interdependent on, which often leads to a consolidation between enterprise members within the enterprise moving to a control-based governance structure (corporatisation) – these are characteristics of a vertically integrated (linked) enterprise. This enterprise structure most closely approximates the traditional vertically integrated company; which however is a single legal entity. In a vertically integrated (linked) enterprise a single, or very few significant members, with a distinct value contribution cover most of the value stream in order to utilise economies of scale and potential for standardisation. The selection of value members is therefore based on their capability to be highly efficient in their operations to compensate for decreasing value propositions of the competencies through the minimisation of transaction costs.

Quadrant 4: Low Current Engage-Ability and Low Future Potential Engage-Ability

Value members found in this quadrant have a prevalence of *enterprise modules* and competencies that are perceived as undesirable for current and future engagement and are value members who own them are confronted with the strategic decision to either disengage from their current structure and search for other new engagements or remain dormant – these are characteristics of a *defunct enterprise*.

Findings show that, once established, inter-organisational relationships and their related enterprise governance structures will have to change over time depending on the varying significance of endogenous and exogenous contingency factors acting upon them. This is in order to stay adaptive to constantly and rapidly changing industrial and inter-organisational relationship requirements, and so become complex adaptive systems that evolve within an 'ecosystem' (Kauffman, 1993). For instance, more stable enterprise governance structures which give more path dependent relationships between *value members* could be used to utilise the existing knowledge base more effectively – what March (1991) calls exploitation (e.g. for producing moderate innovation - without necessarily limiting their adaptability or creating a lock-in situation) whereas links with new *value members* in more flexible governance structures could be used to expand the existing knowledge base – what March (1991) calls exploration – (e.g. to facilitate thinking outside the box and produce radical innovation); Galunic and Eisenhardt (2001) termed this kind of adaptive organisational form a 'dynamic community'.

Based on MacBeth (2002), each of these *enterprise structures* is considered to be in a 'dynamic equilibrium' within the '*collaborative enterprise'* ecosystem around which the *collaborative activities* cluster for a certain period until morphing into another structure (what they call 'bifurcation'). Moreover, these examples show that the bifurcation from one structure to another can follow a two-way pattern (hence the double sided arrows in Figure 11) although the anti-clockwise cyclical pattern from the virtual *(autonomous) enterprise* through the extended *(partner) enterprise* to vertically integrated *(linked) enterprise* is the most common and likely evolution to be observed in practice. This evolutionary change of *enterprise structures* is detailed in Figure 12 in form of a *Dynamic Reference Grid*.

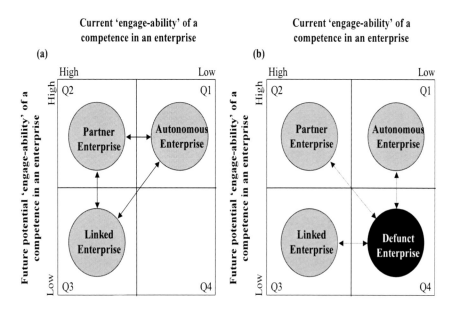

Figure 12. The Dynamic Enterprise Reference Grid (a) planned (b) unplanned reconfiguration of enterprise structures.

It is argued that such reconfiguration actions (as shown in Figure 12a) are largely planned on controllable endogenous contingency aspects that influence the *engage-ability* of competencies (e.g. transaction frequency, sophistication of competence, etc.) whilst unplanned and reactive actions are represented by arrows from and to Quadrant 4 (shown in Figure 12b). These reactive actions are predominantly caused by adverse and uncontrollable exogenous contingency aspects influencing the *engage-ability* of the competencies (e.g. marketability and competition) and should be avoided through better collaborative enterprise management practices.

6.4. GOVERNING ENTERPRISES: A STEP-BY-STEP APPROACH

Governing *collaborative activities* in *enterprises* is like putting together a jigsaw where each bit of the jigsaw (i.e. *enterprise modules*) is owned by a different company. A potted account of how to apply the conceptual elements of the framework is given in Figure 13 followed by a step-by-step approach. The overall deployment of the concept is similar to the main four steps of managing supplier relationships in commonly used portfolio models (e.g. Bensaou, 1999; Kraljic, 1983; Olsen and Ellram, 1997b; Svensson, 2004) such as:

(i)   classify components or activities / analyse business environment
(ii)   classify supply base / analyse of relationship criteria
(iii)   determine appropriate relationship strategy
(iv)   develop action plans / managerial decision of relationship strategy.

However, these approaches are not based upon the premise of an *enterprise*, which is a collection of parts of different companies, and so lack the sophistication of the *collaborative enterprise governance* concept to back them up. This means that the same phenomena will not be detected in any subsequent analysis. Particularly distinguishing is the fact that the *collaborative enterprise governance* concept pays special attention to the issues of building and managing inter-organisational R&D relationships in alignment to the structure-conduct-performance paradigm (Bain, 1956); in the sense that performance of the R&D project and the related inter-organisational relationship depends on the adoption of appropriate suppliers, relationship strategies and structures according to the nature of a particular R&D project's requirements.

1   Identification of a *collaborative activity* to be performed within the *collaborative enterprise*
2   Mapping out the *value members* of the *enterprise* (in terms of their roles) that make an engaging value proposition to the *collaborative activity*; mapping out the *value stream* – the sequence of events from beginning to end that add value to products and services that the *enterprise* delivers

3   Population of the cells in the *Enterprise Matrix* (cf. Figure 10) that deliver information about who (a *value member*) does what (stage of the *value stream*) based on their value proposition to the *collaborative activity*

4   Determine *engage-ability* of *value members* based on transferability, attractiveness and maturity of their competencies (cf. Table 12)

5   Select appropriate *enterprise structure* (i.e. governance strategy) for the *engagement* with the *value members* (cf. Figure 11)

6   Manage the inter-organisational relationships according to the selected governance mode (cf. Table 11)

7   Adapt *enterprise structure* to changing industrial (exogenous) and relationship requirements (endogenous) as moving along the *value stream* based on active contingency planning to sustain competitiveness in the future (cf. Figure 12)

8   Re-populate cells in *Enterprise Matrix* according to changed environmental (exogenous and endogenous) requirements

9   Repeat the above steps on a periodic basis

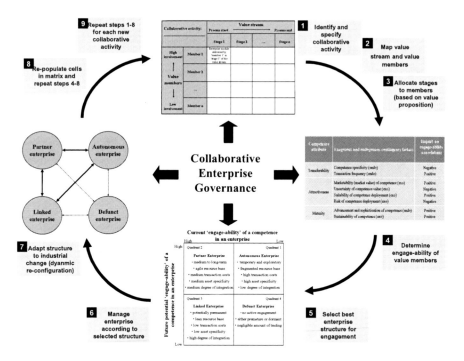

Figure 13. A step-by-step approach of applying the concept of Collaborative Enterprise Governance.

The result is a disciplined approach for sustainable supplier management using the concept of *Collaborative Enterprise Governance*. It thereby does not necessarily seek to make whole-company to whole-company connectivity but concentrates on the criticality of the *enterprise modules* (autonomous parts of collaborating companies) to the whole *enterprise* captured through *collaborative activity*. The concept ensures the optimisation of the overall supply network through the appropriate governance of all dyadic relationships between *enterprise governor* (usually OEM) and involved *value members* (usually suppliers) within the *enterprise*.

6.5. EXAMPLES FROM THE GERMAN AUTOMOTIVE INDUSTRY

To illustrate the *Collaborative Enterprise Governance* concept an empirical example is given in Table 13 to explain how and why *enterprise structures* change. Table 13 shows:

(1) Concepts and principles developed from this research (Column 1 in Table 13)
(2) Empirical examples derived from the interviews (Column 2 in Table 13).

Thereby, different examples are used to explain the static and dynamic components of the concept because this has been a cross-sectional study and not a longitudinal one. However, at an aggregated level it demonstrates the connection between the concept of *Collaborative Enterprise Governance* and the empirical examples representative of inductive grounded reasoning.

Table 13. Provenance of the conceptual framework based on empirical findings and theoretical principles

(1) Conceptualisation of Collaborative Enterprise Governance			(2) Empirical examples
Static	Dynamic	Characteristics	
Q 1 Virtual (Autonomous) Enterprise V(A)E		Flexible, loose, temporary and project based collaborative venture (low degree of integration) Spread risk over many partners (fragmented resource base) Using highly specific but untested competencies (high transaction cost due to high asset specificity)	BMW uses this structure for highly innovative projects and technologies in the early stages of a joint product development process to increase collaboration with small and medium sized companies perceived as being innovative. This happened in the case of BMW's i-drive navigation system, where one small company identified the technology, another company developed the initial concept and another partner conducted the industrialisation of the production-ready product. All the partners were co-ordinated within an autonomous enterprise that was co-ordinated by BMW.
Q 2 Extended (Partner) Enterprise E(P)E		More stable, strategic, close and permanent collaborative venture focused on mutual relationships (medium degree of integration) Risk spread over critical and successful partners (agile resource base) Using matured and tested competencies that are synergistic to collaborative venture (medium transaction cost due to lower asset specificity and less involved partners)	BMW used this structure by engaging more closely with a sole prime contractor (Magna Steyr) for the development and manufacturing of the X3 sport utility vehicle. BMW designed and developed the basic product concept in its mainstream research and development function but then for the medium to long term partnered with Magna Steyr to help orchestrate the large number of sub-suppliers (enterprise management of value members). BMW remained an overall orchestrator or enterprise governor via their purchasing authority.

Table 13. (Continued).

(1) Conceptualisation of Collaborative Enterprise Governance			(2) Empirical examples
Static	Dynamic	Characteristics	
Q 3 Vertically Integrated (Linked) Enterprise VI(L)E		Potentially permanent collaborative venture focused on control and command (high degree of integration) Corporisation of risk through re-intermediation and ownership of assets (lean resource base) Using fully matured, tested and widely accepted competencies (low transaction cost due to low asset specificity)	VW re-designed the structure of its product development process using so called 'Project Houses' (an enterprise module); these are totally autonomous but wholly owned R&D subsidiaries of the main VW organisation. The core organisation covers the design and development of the generic models (e.g. Golf or Passat) and the remaining engineers were re-located to Project Houses competing directly with external suppliers for future development projects of derivate models. This gives VW the option on a fair and planned basis to re-intermediate their position in the enterprise leading to collaboration between the 'basic' organisation and the 'Project Houses' in a linked enterprise.
Q 4 Defunct Enterprise		No active engagement in a current collaborative activity (no degree of integration) Dormant relationship with negligible amount of trading (no transaction cost only data maintenance)	VW kept a supplier for locks in its supply base (stand-by mode) although the company was not competitive anymore due to severe structural and strategic problems. This would contribute towards a defunct enterprise. However, after re-structuring efforts the company's competitiveness and value was re-evaluated and it was re-integrated into the 'active' supply base (i.e. collaborative enterprise) and its collaborative activities.

(1) Conceptualisation of Collaborative Enterprise Governance			(2) Empirical examples
Static	Dynamic	Characteristics	
	Q1 to Q2 From V(A)E to E(P)E	Strategic move for successful ventures depending on existing mutual experiences Effective relationship, technology and knowledge management is critical to establishing common strategies (culture, trust, advanced IT systems, etc.)	The production of the Smart Car, was initially a temporary collaboration with weak ties between parts (enterprise modules) of DaimlerChrysler (DC) and Swatch to exploit temporary market opportunities for very small cars. As the relationship strengthened it became longer term and more permanent.
			This shift in structure was also accompanied by a change in the role of DC, whose role grew from coordinator of manufacturing and logistics operations (relationship and technology management) to include the co-ordination of strategic information (knowledge management). DC acts as an enterprise orchestrator or broker.
	Q2 to Q1 From E(P)E to V(A)E	Successful stable ventures trigger the creation of new temporary ventures Open minded management with pro-active strategies and capabilities in outsourcing is necessary Fulfil a niche or temporary market opportunity requiring a new structure	VW have established partner (and linked) enterprises for conventional product development with partner companies. However, major innovations often require temporary new engagements with companies outside of existing partner enterprises that possess the competencies for newly required technologies. This occurred in the case of the Bugatti Veyron where VW engaged with value members outside its traditional enterprise. This was an example of an new autonomous structure.

Table 13. (Continued).

(1) Conceptualisation of Collaborative Enterprise Governance			(2) Empirical examples
Static	Dynamic	Characteristics	
	Q2 to Q3 From E(P)E to VI(L)E	Often known as the 'shake-out' stage The owners of enterprise modules with predominantly medium asset specific content move to adopt 'lock-in' tactics to gain industrial dominance Involves large financial resources Objective to achieve economies of scale	Due to problems of achieving further market penetration for the Smart Car, tension between DC and Swatch grew and led to the buyout of the two-seated Smart Car from Swatch by DC. This means a transition from a partner enterprise structure towards a linked enterprise structure as major parts of the know-how and competencies of the venture became re-intermediated (or re-insourced) into units of DC. DC became an overwhelmingly dominant force controlling the collaborative relationship that once has been a partner enterprise.
	Q3 to Q2 From VI(L)E to E(P)E	Moving from quadrant 3 to 2 would mean that a new partnership has revived an existing and proven module by deploying it in a new partner enterprise	For the Smart Car, DC deployed its core competencies in other new directions, for example the production of the new Smart Forfour car jointly designed by Mitsubishi in another separate inter-company activity where 50% of the parts are supplied by Mitsubishi and the engines are supplied by another German-Japanese venture involving Mercedes-Benz forming a partner enterprise that spans the whole product life cycle across company boundaries.

(1) Conceptualisation of Collaborative Enterprise Governance			(2) Empirical examples
Static	Dynamic	Characteristics	
	Q3 to Q1 From VI(L)E to V(A)E	Owners of linked enterprise modules that are based on proven competencies should not become complacent but seek new innovative ventures to remain competitive; this could take place in form of a new spin-off enterprise Increasing profitability and competitiveness as main goals for new links (shareholder value maximisation)	Ford span off its wholly owned internal component suppliers (an enterprise module of the Ford organisation) into a new organisation called Visteon that depends less on being a sole supplier to Ford. Ford's new relationship to Visteon is on the basis of an autonomous enterprise. As a result Visteon has grown in volume and competence by also supplying other OEMs, becoming more focussed and specialised. Ford's return on capital employed in the relationship grew as Visteon assets disappeared from its accounts and lower prices arose from increased innovation throughout the enterprise.
	Q1 to Q3 From V(A)E to VI(L)E	In case of attractive, highly asset specific and complementary competencies, a former partner can strive to control those assets internally Aiming at in-house development of proprietary systems, e.g. through acquisition of external competencies, to lower transaction cost	In 2002, the engineering service provider IVM was acquired by the Edscha Group (a large systems supplier who specialises in convertible roofs) and integrated as an autonomous business unit, i.e. enterprise module, (keeping its own company name) so that IVM's research and development competencies could be deployed internally with lower transaction costs.
		Objective of extending business portfolio to cover whole product life cycle	It also enables Edscha to offer a comprehensive service package (e.g. design, development, manufacturing, delivery and assembly) not only for convertible roofs but gradually for whole cars drawing on IVM's design and development expertise. This could increase the Edscha Group's future potential to rise towards the role of an orchestrator itself by becoming more influential.

6.6. SUMMARY

This Chapter presents a novel competence based contingency framework that addresses the empirical observations and challenges in inter-organisational relationship governance. This was accomplished by the development of the concept of *Collaborative Enterprise Governance* with the following key characteristics:

- Individual companies are conceptualised as a nexus of autonomous *enterprise modules* that deliver competencies to *collaborative activities* in *enterprises* thereby combining issues of internal and external coordination.
- The investigation and collection of data about *collaborative activities* is facilitated by the *Enterprise Matrix* tool that helps map the *value members* along the *value stream* of the *collaborative activity.*
- The decision of involvement in a *collaborative activity* of an *enterprise* depends on the *engage-ability* of the respective competencies of the *value members.* Thereby, the selection of an appropriate inter-organisational governance structure (i.e. *enterprise structure)* is contingent upon three main competence attributes (transferability, attractiveness and maturity). These have been parsimoniously summarised in the *Dynamic Enterprise Reference Grid* identifying three major *enterprise structures,* i.e. vitual *(autonomous) enterprise*, extended *(partner) enterprise*, and vertically integrated *(linked) enterprise.*
- The structures and their related relationships are, however, constantly changing and reiterating through evolutionary enterprise configuration in order to stay adaptive to changes of exogenous (external to relationship) and endogenous (internal to relationship) requirements and hence to sustain competitiveness.
- This requires dynamic and flexible *enterprise governance* based on the active contingency planning of controllable endogenous factors.

Empirical examples were given to illustrate the static and dynamic elements of the *Collaborative Enterprise Governance* concept explaining how and why *enterprise structures* change. This was finally merged into a potted account of how the elements of the concept should be applied in a step-by-step approach.

## Chapter 7

PRACTICAL IMPLICATIONS –
LEADING THE 3RD REVOLUTION

"It's not a panacea, but collaboration can be the differentiator that gives one supply chain the edge over another" (Forger, 2000; p. 97)

In the previous Chapter 6 a novel conceptual contingency framework was presented in the context of sustainable supplier management. It is embedded in the empirical context of R&D collaboration in the German automotive industry and tries to close the identified gap between theory and practice on the topic of inter-organisational relationship governance through theory extension based on insights gained from extensive empirical field work.

However, one aspect of inter-organisational relationship governance remains uncovered: its impact on sustainable competitive success. This involves the identification of the usability and practicality of the developed concept and its impact on the success of the whole partnership, i.e. *enterprise*, and its *value members*. This was pursued by conducting a focus group in form of an industrial workshop with experts from the German automotive industry.

7.1. IMPACT OF SUSTAINABLE
SUPPLIER MANAGEMENT ON NETWORK SUCCESS

Based on the empirical findings and their validation, we argue that applying the *Collaborative Enterprise Governance* concept can lead to a sustainable competitive success. However, one of the biggest problems in this context is the actual measurement of the performance of R&D projects, because it is difficult to allocate all costs and benefits to the inter-organisational R&D project and its partners properly. Otto and Kotzab (2003) suggest using attained goals to measure 'competitive priorities' whilst others (e.g. Corbett and Van Wassenhove, 1993; Hult *et al.*, 2006; Mohr and Spekman, 1994) suggests that three performance measures should be directly linked to the success of inter-organisational R&D relationships on the project level: *time*, *quality* and *cost*.

In Figure 14 below *time* is described in % project completion, *quality* is described in % problems / defects, and *cost* is described in % total target cost. Figure 14 depicts that:

- changes in the supply base (i.e. switching suppliers) due to a supplier selection based on short-term orientated cost criteria rather than long-term orientated total value creation
- a late and insufficient involvement of suppliers in the development process
- a lack of open communication and information sharing (characteristics of the still prevailing sourcing practice)

have a negative impact on the competitiveness of the R&D project and its relationship. This is due to emerging time delays, quality and maturity problems and higher cost to compensate for these problems and unplanned changes in order to meet the agreed start of production (SOP) deadline. Thereby, the later the changes take place the more severe the impact will be (symbolised by the length of the arrows in Figure 14). Furthermore, it became evident that the reasons for supplier switches change as the project moves along the development stages. For "during the early concept stages technology and innovation issues are drivers for supplier switches, in the later stages quality and time issues are more important" (Specialist Engineer Design Car Body, OEM). Paradoxically, this increases the dilemma of time delays, quality problems and cost increase leading to a vicious circle of supplier switches and loss of R&D efficiency.

This supports the empirically grounded argument that establishing and institutionalising sustainable supplier management, by applying the *Collaborative Enterprise Governance* concept, is an effective means to reduce costs and development time of R&D projects in the short-term as well as to improve quality and innovation output in the long-term, not only for the individual *value member* but also for the whole *enterprise*.

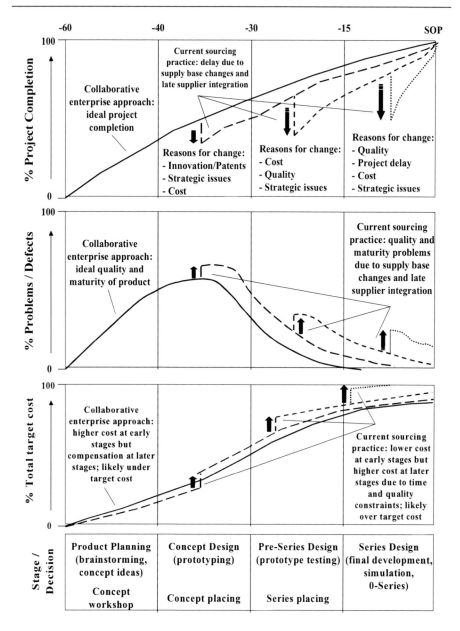

Figure 14. Impact of *Collaborative Enterprise Governance* on time, quality and cost of R&D projects.

Major aspects that facilitate this causality, thereby confirming and building on key features of *Collaborative Enterprise Governance*, were identified by the industrial experts as:

- Quick and early problem solving through early collaboration

"We agree that errors occur early during the development stages and that if you work well at these stages you will get the benefit at the end. However, this is hard to measure and hence difficult to argue" (R&D Director, Module supplier).

- Less opportunistic behaviour off all partners through mutual safeguards and strategic thinking

"The supplier accepts the target price which the OEM has calculated in his cost estimation. Therefore, the supplier is involved from the beginning and has a certain planning stability" (R&D Director, Module Supplier).

- Risk and reward sharing

"You will be more likely to invest into a new product line if you have an OEM in the background that wants to this together with you" (Group Leader Design, Systems Supplier).
"Often you have a competent partner that is not necessarily lean, i.e. there is a potential for mutually optimising processes and structures. The savings should then be equally shared" (Specialist Engineer Design Car Body, OEM).

- Increased communication and information sharing

"In product development it is the question how to get the knowledge to the supplier. Thereby, trust as well as open and constant communication are the key factors to achieve this. Only then both parties will benefit" (Specialist Engineer Design Car Body, OEM).

- No switching cost through competent leadership

"Experience shows that our current approach is normally very expensive, because you have to re-negotiate for unplanned changes, eventually switch suppliers shortly before SOP, develop new tooling, change concepts, etc. This could be avoided with such a collaborative approach. But therefore we need to move away from being multi-project managers and become engineers again" (Manager Project Integration, OEM).

- Joint definition of product and process specifications with clearly defined responsibilities

"For a long-term partnership it is important that you clearly define the component and its functionality. Then, you need to transfer this information to the supplier and integrate the supplier in the development of the detailed specification and task catalogue for this part" (Manager Design Car Body, OEM).
- Convergent expectations and goals through holistic thinking

"Of course we transfer the quality requirements of the OEMs onto our sub-suppliers because only then the quality of the final product can be assured" (Group Leader Design, Systems Supplier).
- Higher responsiveness through strong integration

"When we worked on the Z8 with BMW we had to change the position of the lock in the very last minute. This did only work out in the end because we had a good and close working relationship with BMW" (Group Leader Design, Systems Supplier).

Similar aspects in the context of general benefits of good collaboration practice in inter-organisational relationships and co-development projects can be found in the existing literature (e.g. Dyer and Singh, 1998; Maloni and Benton, 2000; Mohr and Spekman, 1994; Primo and Amundson, 2002).

7.2. TOWARDS SUSTAINABLE SUPPLIER MANAGEMENT

The above evidence and discussion confirms that the majority of companies in the (German) automotive industry are unfortunately not predominantly thinking about sustainable supplier management or *Collaborative Enterprise Governance*. But as mentioned above, especially in times of economic crisis and drastically changing customer requirements sustainable supplier management is essential in order to be successful. To help car makers and their suppliers towards sustainable supplier management practice we have put together a list of recommendations. Similar, although more general, suggestions can be found in the inter-organisational relationship literature (e.g. Ballou *et al.*, 2000; Handfield and Bechtel, 2002; Swink and Mabert, 2000).

For OEMs

- Commitment to suppliers - an early and long-term commitment (ideally with guaranteed return business for suppliers over vehicle life time) will allow for long term planning of suppliers and in return will lead to higher ownership commitment towards cost, quality and innovation
- Open book accounting - the target price of each product should include a mutually agreed profit margin for the suppliers that is assured and that is not affected by any re-negotiations for unplanned changes
- Life cycle costing - OEMs need to start thinking strategically in terms of the whole life cycle costs of a product (e.g. including cost for warranty) rather than just the short-term R&D costs upfront
- Open communication and information sharing - design data in form of drawings and CAD data should be shared with the suppliers as well as time schedules for development and production processes, production volume data, etc. in order to allow the supplier to get a bigger picture of all the aspects involved
- Leadership - OEMs need to pursue the role of the leader and coordinator within inter-organisational R&D projects with the clear authority of final decision making. Therefore, they need to increase the speed and quality of their decision making to ensure a more effective and efficient project and interface management
- Balancing internal and external knowhow - as collaboration (especially within the R&D process) is based on the exchange of technical knowhow, it is inevitable that the OEMs build up a sufficient level of product specific technical competencies (not only relationship specific social competencies) in order to manage the interfaces between the partners and their knowhow effectively
- Balanced supply base - for their sourcing strategies OEMs need to take into consideration product attributes (e.g. complex system, standard commodity, innovative and differentiating product, etc.) as well as supplier attributes (e.g. R&D competence, high quality, low cost, etc.) when selecting an appropriate supplier for collaboration

leading to a balanced supply base for different types of constellations and requirements

- Customer focus - OEMs need to be aware of customer needs and requirements and have to translate these into technical functionalities and specifications for the suppliers in order to develop innovative products that also fulfil generic category benefits at important customer interfaces, i.e. areas that matter to the customer

- Boundary spanning - it can be argued that transforming the traditional role of purchasing into a more strategic sourcing function might not be sufficient to achieve real cross-boundary collaboration but that a dedicated alliance function acting as an 'Ombudsman' (Handfield and Bechtel, 2002) between OEM and suppliers is necessary. This does not necessarily need to be a single person but could involve an independent cross-functional and inter-organisational R&D committee of OEM and suppliers.

For Suppliers

- Ownership - suppliers are required to take more ownership in the product development and play a more active role during inter-organisational R&D projects, e.g. through investments in testing and tooling (customer-specific assets), active commitment towards quality goals, meeting negotiated requirements such as target price, etc.

- Offer exclusivity - in return for early and long-term commitment with potential return business of the OEM (see above) the supplier should offer the OEM exclusive rights to the innovation and not aim at standardising this part among as many OEMs as possible

- Organisational adaptation - suppliers need to adjust their organisational structure and processes to be adaptive to the increased requirements of inter-firm R&D relationships, particularly on the systems and module level (e.g. creation of customer specific key account management)

- Sub-supplier management - because inter-organisational R&D collaboration is increasingly carried out on the more complex systems and module levels suppliers (especially 1st tiers) do not possess the competence for all sub-parts in-house and therefore need to develop skills (relationship-specific assets) for effectively and efficiently

managing their sub-suppliers in accordance to the overall project
requirements

- Information sharing - suppliers also need to be willing to share their
  information (especially cost information) with the OEMs in a
  transparent manner
- Total process partner - suppliers should increase their efforts to
  identify future technological trends and developments (independent
  from the OEMs) based on end consumer desires and requirements
- Physical proximity - local or regional presence and proximity to the
  OEM can facilitate face-to-face contact in critical phases of R&D
  projects.

The fundamental root of all this is the development of trust in each other
to safeguard the transactions from opportunistic behaviour of the individual
partners (e.g. Dyer, 1996c; Johnston *et al.*, 2004; Monczka *et al.*, 1998). Both
sides need to overcome bad experiences from the past and move on in an
unbiased and unprejudiced way (*tabula rasa*). Furthermore, the automotive
industry on the macro level needs to focus on high technology and innovation
rather than price dumping which should be reflected in the business behaviour
within and between firms (e.g. through the adoption of *Collaborative
Enterprise Governance).* However, although the terminology reflecting
Collaborative Enterprise Governance (cf. Binder *et al.*, 2008) is commonly
used in the automotive industry, the underlying philosophy is not widely
recognised. Hence, it is inevitable that aspects of partnerships and
collaborative inter-organisational relationships are considered more thoroughly
in the future in order to become and remain competitive.

7.3. SUMMARY

This chapter reported on the validation of the implications of
Collaborative Enterprise Governance on the sustainable competitive success
of *enterprises* and their *value members* through a focus group exercise with
industrial experts from the German automotive industry. It revealed that the
use of *Collaborative Enterprise Governance* to design *enterprises* and manage
their *collaborative activities* between the *value members* can lead to the
realisation of sustainable competitive success in terms of faster development
time, higher quality, and lower development cost in R&D projects.
Nevertheless, current practice in the German automotive industry is still not

reflecting the idea of *Collaborative Enterprise Governance* and is hence facing major challenges on its way to a distinct European governance model based on partnership-focused collaborative relationships. Various principles have been suggested to help *enterprise governors* and *value members* (i.e. OEMs and suppliers) on their way to adopt the *Collaborative Enterprise Governance* concept. Only then will the 3rd revolution within the automotive industry, driven by collaboration, be successful in the long term.

Chapter 8

CONCLUSION

"The supplier that is captured in cost-slavery does not deliver innovation, but the supplier with sufficient degrees of freedom to innovate; hence, the key to success lies within strategic supplier management" (Dudenhöffer, 2003; p. 4).

The omnipresent global economic crisis has had a particularly dramatic effect on the global automotive industry. It has increased the need for a 3rd revolution and the move towards mass-collaboration between all industrial players; that may ultimately lead to a governance model based on partnership-focused collaborative relationships. The first two revolutions were led by the US and Japan respectively, but we propose that this time, the European automotive industry will lead the way in the 3rd revolution. This is based evidence about how the industry in trying to restructure, change practices and behaviour since the late 1990s.

In this book we have looked at some potential survival measures from an operations and supply chain management perspective focusing on the issue of sustainable supplier management. In this context an empirical study conducted in the German automotive industry provides insights that for long term sustainable improvements. Inter-organisational R&D collaborations must be improved by establishing a more intense collaboration between car makers and their suppliers early in the product development process. This should be achievable through:

- an early and intense involvement of key suppliers
- an open and intense sharing of know how between the project partners
- a long-term orientation towards inter-firm R&D relationships

- an involvement of multiple cross-functional interfaces and clearly defined responsibilities
- an existence of a competent leader within the supply network who manages the interfaces between the project partners.

Thereby, the sustainable success of the inter-organisational R&D collaboration is based on competence rather than cost issues which results in a cost, time and quality improvements for the overall supply network; an effect that should be of general interest to all automotive companies, whether they are car manufacturers or suppliers.

This inductive research extends the current literature by not focusing on the individual firm's strategy or on the traditional supply chain view, but instead focussing on developmental issues at the *enterprise* (i.e. supply network) level. It unites exogenous and endogenous theories of the firm from an inter-disciplinary body of knowledge. Merging these with empirical evidence from the German automotive industry, it delivers unique strategic insights about designing and managing collaborative practice. This should be of interest to students of strategic management, scholars and practitioners who are aiming to design and manage enterprises more effectively.

The novel *Collaborative Enterprise Governance* methodology described in this chapter considers an *enterprise* to be made up of *modules* (parts) of different companies. Each *module* is built around highly specific competencies, such as proprietary technology, and is integrated with other *modules* using less specific capabilities and resources, such as shared information and process technology. By taking this unique approach in analysing the industrial environment, and its dynamics, it has been possible to identify a suitable *enterprise structure* for different collaborative settings based on the prevailing type of competence. In summary, four different types of *enterprise structures* and four different types of core competencies have been parsimoniously characterised and a two-way dependency proposed between each respective pairing. Core competencies with:

- low current but high future engage-ability are associated with *virtual (autonomous) enterprise structures*
- high current and high future engage-ability are associated with *extended (partner) enterprise structures,*
- high current but decreasing future engage-ability are associated with *vertically integrated (linked) enterprise structures* and

- low current and low future engage-ability are associated with *defunct enterprise structures*.

The conceptual framework of *Collaborative Enterprise Governance* for a sustainable supplier management is supported by extant literature and new empirical data evident in the German automotive industry. However, we do not claim that all inter-organisational relationships follow this behaviour. Neither is it claimed that a deterministic relationship exists between *enterprise structure* and the prevailing type of core competence, as it is only probabilistic. We only claim that a dependency is observable and that behaviour is driven by a combination of exogenous and endogenous factors as defined by current literature. Furthermore the research has not only determined the positive effect of *Collaborative Enterprise Governance* but has also led to the development of specific guidelines for practitioners (OEMs and suppliers) on changes that are necessary to make *Collaborative Enterprise Governance* a reality and supplier relationships increasingly sustainable.

Thereby the novel *Collaborative Enterprise Governance* framework extends current literature based on the following theoretical contributions:

- *Collaborative Enterprise Governance* presents a holistic and integrated concept of sustainable inter-organisational relationship governance by using the dyadic relationship (embedded in its network context reflected by a joint R&D project) as unit of competitive analysis (total system optimisation)
- *Collaborative Enterprise Governance* establishes the important link between product, process and supply structures by combining issues of SCM and Product Development Management based on the establishment of the *Enterprise Matrix* as tool to coordinate joint R&D projects
- At the core of *Collaborative Enterprise Governance* lies a portfolio ideology for strategic sourcing at the early stages of R&D collaboration that builds on value based thinking by drawing on competencies as main contingency. Thereby, the contingent fit (i.e. *engage-ability*) between different types of governance modes for a relationship (i.e. *enterprise structures*) and different types of competencies of the partners in a relationship has been parsimoniously characterised and a two-way dependency
- *Collaborative Enterprise Governance* introduces modular thinking by conceptualising an individual partner company as a set of autonomous

cross-functional units (*enterprise modules*) that contain all necessary competencies to fulfil a certain task within a joint R&D project. It thereby combines issues of internal and external collaboration based on part-to-part rather than company-to-company connectivity

- *Collaborative Enterprise Governance* considers dynamic aspects of adapting and reconfiguring relationship strategies and governance structures based on active execution of management roles and activities.

A limitation to this research is its cross-sectional character. The inter-organisational R&D relationship aspects in the German automotive industry have been studied at certain discrete points of time which can only provide static snapshots rather than dynamic longitudinal insights. This particularly limits the causal predictions of the concept in the sense that no deterministic causality can be derived on how governance structures re-configure over time but only a probabilistic dependency can be proposed.

Furthermore, the focus on competence as single contingency factor for the governance of inter-organisational relationships despite its virtue of parsimony can be seen as a limitation. An implication of this is that there will be cases and instances in inter-organisational relationship governance in which other factors, such as historically grown situations, capacity utilisation, political factors, etc., play a major role that cannot be explained by the contingency upon competencies.

Current research is replicating this study based in different countries and further research will focus on inter-organisational relationships and *collaborative enterprise structures*, using a first tier supplier as the *enterprise integrator* (Johnsen and Ford, 2005) rather than an OEM. This is because trends point to first tier *enterprise* members taking on more and more responsibility for managing supply logistics, design, and sub-assembly integration, which will inevitably make them become more powerful. This is demonstrated by the takeover of the Opel (the German part of GM company) by the Austro-Canadian supplier Magna in mid 2009. Another possibility for future research in this area is to focus upon unsustainable inter-organisational relationships (Anderson and Jap, 2005), which have been identified as existing by this study (depicted as '*defunct enterprises*') but have not yet been fully investigated (e.g. the collapse of MG Rover or DaimlerChrysler).

GLOSSARY

The terms explained below reflect the specific terminology used in the context of the novel *Collaborative Enterprise Governance* concept described in Chapter 6 of this book.

(Collaborative) Enterprise:	An entity, regardless of its legal form, including partnerships or associations regularly engaged in economic activities.
Enterprise Module:	An autonomous cross-functional part of an individual company consisting of highly task specific competencies that determine its value proposition complemented by lower task specific relational interface capabilities that enable the unique competence to be deployed within a collaborative activity of an enterprise.
Collaborative activity:	A collaborative activity is a joint business activity between value members in an enterprise and can involve a product, a service, or a project consisting of certain value adding tasks that are fulfilled by the value members that possess the most appropriate value proposition.
Value stream:	The value stream is a collection of tasks that have to be fulfilled along the product development stages within a collaborative activity.

Enterprise (Value) Member:	Individual companies consisting of one or more enterprise modules that contribute value through the delivery of their competencies to one or more specific tasks of a collaborative activity within an enterprise.
Engage-ability:	Engage-ability determines the ability of a value member to be involved in a collaborative activity based on its value proposition.
Value proposition:	Value proposition is the potential of a value member to create a distinct value for an enterprise based on the transferability, attractiveness, and maturity of its competencies.
Enterprise Governor:	The leader of an enterprise who possesses the meta-competence for enterprise design and management.
Meta-competence:	Capability of evaluating the enterprise modules of the value members, allocating suitable modules to tasks of the collaborative activity, and defining the responsibilities of and boundaries between the collaborating value members.
Enterprise Design:	Enterprise design involves the evaluation of potential value members for participation in an enterprise, the allocation of the value member to tasks in the collaborative activity, and the selection of an appropriate relationship strategy and structure with the value member based on its engage-ability.
Enterprise Structure:	An enterprise structure reflects the specific relationship strategy and structure between the enterprise governor and a value member and can be characterised in terms of depth, scope, longevity, proximity, and governance style.

Enterprise Management:	Enterprise management involves facilitating the collaboration between value members and between the value members and the enterprise governor (in case of delegation of the enterprise management to a significant value member), i.e. coordinating the delivery of competencies to tasks of the collaborative activity.
Sustainable Enterprise Competitiveness:	Sustainable enterprise competitiveness is related to a superior value proposition of the enterprise to the customer that competing enterprises cannot adopt. It emerges from the integration of individual value members' competencies through effective and efficient enterprise design and management.

REFERENCES

A.T. Kearney (2003), "Annual Automotive Study 2003", *Study*, Düsseldorf.

A.T. Kearney (2004), "Produktentwicklungsprozess als Schlüssel zur Kostenführerschaft" [Product development process as key to cost leadership], *Study*, Düsseldorf.

Amit, R. and Schoemaker, P.J.H. (1993), "Strategic assets and organizational rent", *Strategic Management Journal*, Vol. 14, No. 2, pp. 33-46.

Anderson, E. and Jap, S.D. (2005), "The dark side of close relationships", *MIT Sloan Management Review*, Spring, pp. 75-82.

Anderson, J.C., Hakansson, H. and Johanson, J. (1994), "Dyadic business relationships within a business network context", *Journal of Marketing*, Vol. 58, October, pp. 1-15.

Arthur D. Little (2005), "Wachstumsfinanzierung in der Automobilzulieferindustrie" [Growth investment in the automotive supplier industry], *Study*, Wiesbaden.

Auerbach, C.F. and Silverstein, L.B. (2003), *Qualitative Data: An Introduction to Coding and Analysis*, New York University Press, New York.

Babbage, C. (1835), *On the Economy of Machinery and Manufacturing*, 4th ed., London, Reprint: 1971 New York.

Bain, J.S. (1956), *Barriers to New Competition*, Harvard University Press, Cambridge.

Baines, T.S. and Kay, G. (2002), "Manufacturing sourcing practices and relationships", *The International Journal of Logistics Management*, Vol. 13, No. 2, pp. 101-113.

Baines, T.S., Whitney, D.E. and Fines, C. (1999), "Manufacturing technology sourcing practices in the USA", *International Journal of Production Research*, Vol. 37, No. 4, pp. 939-956.

Baldwin, C.Y. and Clark, K.B. (1997), "Managing in an age of modularity", *Harvard Business Review*, September-October, pp. 84-93.

Baldwin, C.Y. and Clark, K.B. (2006a), "Modularity in the design of complex engineering systems", in: Minai, A., Braha, D. and Bar Yam, Y. (Eds.), *Complex Engineered Systems: Science Meets Technology,* New England Complex Systems Institute Series on Complexity, Springer-Verlag, New York.

Baldwin, C.Y. and Clark, K.B. (2006b), "Where do transactions come from? A network design perspective on the theory of the firm", *Harvard Business School Working Paper*, No. 06-051, pp. 1-45.

Ballou, R.H., Gilbert, S.M. and Mukherjee, A. (2000), "New managerial challenges form supply chain opportunities", *Industrial Marketing Management*, Vol. 29, No. 1, pp. 7-18.

Barley, S.R. (2006), "When I write my masterpiece: thoughts on what makes a paper interesting", *Academy of Management Journal*, Vol. 49, No. 1, pp. 16-20.

Barney, J.B. (1991), "Firm resources and sustained competitive advantage", *Journal of Management*, Vol. 17, No. 1, pp. 99-120.

Barney, J.B., Wright, M. and Ketchen Jr., D.J. (2001), "The resource-based view of the firm: ten years after 1991", *Journal of Management*, Vol. 27, No. 6, pp. 625-641.

Barwise, P. and Meehan, S. (2004), "Don't be unique, be better", *MIT Sloan Management Review*, Summer, pp. 23-26.

Bates, H., Holweg, M., Lewis, M. and Oliver, N. (2007), "Motor vehicle recalls: trends, pattern and emerging issues", *OMEGA – The International Journal of Management Science*, Vol. 35, No. 2, 202-210.

Becker, M.C. and Zirpoli, F. (2003), Organizing new product development: knowledge hollowing-out and knowledge integration – the Fiat auto case", *International Journal of Operations & Production Management*, Vol. 23, No. 9, pp. 1033-1061.

Becker, W. and Dietz, J. (2004), "R&D cooperation and innovation activities of firms – evidence for the German manufacturing industry", *Research Policy*, Vol. 33, No. 2, pp. 209-223.

Bensaou, M. (1999), "Portfolios of buyer-supplier relationships", *Sloan Management Review,* Summer, pp. 35-44.

Bettis, R.A. (1998), "Commentary on 'Redefining industry structure for the information age' by J.L. Sampler", *Strategic Management Journal*, Vol. 19, No. 4, pp. 357-361.

Binder, M. and Clegg, B.T. (2005), "The modular enterprise: a new governance architecture for inter-firm collaboration", *Proceedings of the 12th International Annual EurOMA Conference*, Corvinus University, Budapest, 19-22 June, pp. 1385-1394.

Binder, M. and Clegg, B.T. (2006), "A conceptual framework for enterprise management", *International Journal of Production Research*, Vol. 44, Nos. 18/19, pp. 3813-3829.

Binder, M. and Clegg, B.T. (2007), "Enterprise management: a new frontier for organisations", *International Journal of Production Economics*, (in press).

Binder, M. and Edwards, J.S. (2010), "Using grounded theory method for theory building in operations management research: A study on inter-firm relationship governance", *International Journal of Operations & Production Management*, Vol. 30, No. 3 (to appear).

Binder, M., Gust, P. and Clegg, B.T. (2008), "The importance of collaborative frontloading in automotive supply networks", *Journal of Manufacturing Technology Management*, Vol. 19, No. 3, pp. 315-331.

Bititci, U.S., Martinez, V., Albores, P. and Mendibil, K. (2003), "Creating and sustaining competitive advantage in collaborative systems: the what and the how", *Production Planning & Control*, Vol. 14, No. 5, pp. 410-424.

Bititci, U.S., Martinez, V., Albores, P. and Parung, J. (2004), "Creating and managing value in collaborative networks", *International Journal of Physical Distribution & Logistics Management*, Vol. 34, Nos. 3/4, pp. 251-268.

Boardman, J.T. and Clegg, B.T. (2001), "Structured engagement in the extended enterprise", *International Journal of Operations & Production Management*, Vol. 21, Nos. 5/6, pp. 795-811.

Borys, B. and Jemison, D.B. (1989), "Hybrid arrangements as strategic alliances: theoretical issues in organizational combinations", *Academy of Management Review*, Vol. 14, No. 2, pp. 234-249.

Bowersox, D.J., Closs, D.J. and Stank, T.P. (2000), "Ten mega-trends that will revolutionize supply chain logistics", *Journal of Business Logistics*, Vol. 21, No. 2, pp. 1-16.

Briscoe, G., Dainty, A.R.J. and Millet, S. (2001), "Construction supply chain partnerships: skills, knowledge and attitudinal requirements", *European Journal of Purchasing & Supply Management*, Vol. 7, No. 4, pp. 243-255.

Bruner, R. and Spekman, R. (1998), "The dark side of alliances: lessons from Volvo-Renault", *European Management Journal*, Vol. 16, No. 2, pp. 136-150.

Bryman, A. (2004), *Social Research Methods*, 2nd ed., Oxford University Press, New York.

Bullinger, H.-J., Auernhammer, K. and Gomeringer, A. (2004), "Managing innovation networks in the knowledge-driven economy", *International Journal of Production Research*, Vol. 42, No. 17, pp. 3337-3353.

Burgess, K., Singh, P.J. and Koroglu, R. (2006), "Supply chain management: a structured literature review and implications for future research", *International Journal of Operations & Production Management*, Vol. 26, No. 7, pp. 703-729.

Byrne, J.A. and Brandt, R. (1993), "The virtual corporation", *Business Week*, February 8, pp. 36 – 41.

Calabrese, G. (2001), "Editorial: Buyer-supplier partnerships in product development and innovation technology", *International Journal of Automotive Technology and Management*, Vol. 1, Nos. 2/3, pp. 161-168.

Camps, T., Diederen, P., Hofstede, G.J. and Vos, B. (2004), *The Emerging World of Chains and Networks: Bridging Theory and Practice*, Reed Business Information, Gravenhage.

Camuffo, A. (2001), "Rolling out a 'World Car': globalisation, outsourcing and modularity in the auto industry", *IMVP Working Paper*, available at: http://imvp.mit.edu/papers.

Carter, C.R. (2005), "Purchasing social responsibility and firm performance: the key mediating roles of organizational learning and supplier performance", *International Journal of Physical Distribution & Logistics Management*, Vol. 35, No. 3, pp. 177-194.

Chen, I.J. and Paulraj, A. (2004), "Understanding supply chain management: critical research and a theoretical framework", *International Journal of Production Research*, Vol. 42, No. 1, pp. 131-163.

Chesbrough, H.W. and Teece, D.J. (1996), "Organizing for innovation: when is virtual virtuous?", *Harvard Business Review*, January – February, pp. 65-73.

Chiesa, V. and Toletti, G. (2004), "Network of collaborations for innovation: the case of biotechnology", *Technology Analysis & Strategic Management*, Vol. 16, No. 1, pp. 73-96.

Chiesa, V., Manzini, R. and Tecilla, F. (2000), "Selecting sourcing strategies for technological innovation: an empirical case study", *International*

Journal of Operations & Production Management, Vol. 20, No. 9, pp. 1017-1037.

Choi, T.Y. and Krause, D.R. (2006), "The supply base and its complexity: implications for transaction costs, risks, responsiveness, and innovation", *Journal of Operations Management*, Vol. 24, No. 5, pp. 637-652.

Christopher, M. (1998), *Logistics and Supply Chain Management*, Prentice Hall, Englewood Cliffs.

Clegg, B.T. and Binder, M. (2004), "New thoughts on changing enterprise structures: vertical, virtual and extended", *Proceedings of the 11th International Annual EurOMA Conference*, INSEAD, Fontainebleau, 27-29 June, Vol. 1, pp. 125-134.

Coase, R. (1937), "The nature of the firm", *Economica*, Vol. 4, pp. 386-405.

Cohen, W. and Levinthal, D. (1990), "Absorptive capacity: a new perspective on learning and innovation", *Administrative Science Quarterly*, Vol. 35, No. 1, pp. 129–152.

Cooper, M.C., Ellram, L.M., Gardner, J.T. and Hanks, A.M. (1997b), "Meshing multiple alliances", *Journal of Business Logistics*, Vol. 18, No. 1, pp. 67-89.

Cooper, M.C., Lambert, D.M. and Pagh, J.D. (1997a), "Supply chain management: more than a new name for logistics", *The International Journal of Logistics Management*, Vol. 8, No. 1, pp. 1-13.

Corbett, C. and Van Wassenhove, L. (1993), "Trade-offs? What trade-off? Competence and competitiveness in manufacturing strategy", *California Management Review*, Summer, pp. 107-122.

Cousins, P.D. (2002), "A conceptual model for managing long-term inter-organisational relationships", *European Journal of Purchasing & Supply Management*, Vol. 8, No. 2, pp. 71-82.

Cousins, P.D. and Crone, M.J. (2003), "Strategic models for the development of obligation based inter-firm relationships: A study of the UK automotive industry", *International Journal of Operations & Production Management*, Vol. 23, No. 11, pp. 1447-1474.

Cousins, P.D. and Stanwix, E. (2001), "It's only a matter of confidence! A comparison of relationship management of Japanese- and UK non-Japanese-owned vehicle manufacturers", *International Journal of Operations & Production Management*, Vol. 21, No. 9, pp. 1160-1179.

Cousins, P.D., Lawson, B. and Squire, B. (2006), "An empirical taxonomy of purchasing functions", *International Journal of Operations & Production Management*, Vol. 26, No. 7, pp. 775-794.

Coyne, K.P. (1986), "Sustainable competitive advantage – what it is, what it isn't", Business Horizon, January-February, pp. 54-61.

Croom, S., Romano, P. and Giannakis, M. (2000), "Supply chain management: an analytical framework for critical literature review", *European Journal of Purchasing & Supply Management*, Vol. 6, No. 1, pp. 67-83.

Croom, S.R. (2001), "The dyadic capabilities concept: examining the process of key supplier involvement in collaborative product development", *European Journal of Purchasing & Supply Management*, Vol. 7, No. 1, pp. 29-37.

Cusumano, M.A. and Takeishi, A. (1991), "Supplier relations and management: a survey of Japanese, Japanese-transplant, and U.S. auto plants", *Strategic Management Journal*, Vol. 12, No. 8, pp. 563-588.

D'Aveni, R.A. (1994), *Hyper-competition – Managing the Dynamics of Strategic Manoeuvring*, Free Press, New York.

Das, A., Narasimhan, R. and Talluri, S. (2006), "Supplier integration – finding an optimal configuration", *Journal of Operations Management*, Vol. 24, No. 5, pp. 563-582.

Das, T.K. and Teng, B.-S. (2000), "A resource-based theory of strategic alliances", *Journal of Management*, Vol. 26, No. 1, pp. 31-61.

Davidow, W.H. and Malone, M.S. (1992), *The Virtual Corporation: Structuring and Revitalizing the Corporation for the 21st Century*, Harper Collins, New York.

Davis, E.W. and Spekman R.E. (2003), *The Extended Enterprise: Gaining Competitive Advantage Through Collaborative Supply Chains*, Financial Times Prentice Hall, London.

De Toni and Tonchia (2003), "Strategic planning and firms' competencies: traditional approaches and new perspectives", *International Journal of Operations & Production Management*, Vol. 23, No. 9, pp. 947-976.

Doran, D. (2003), "Supply chain implications of modularisation", *International Journal of Operations & Production Management*, Vol. 23, No. 3, pp. 316-326.

Drago, W.A. (1997), "When strategic alliances make sense", *Industrial Management & Data Systems*, Vol. 97, No. 2, pp. 53-57.

Draulans, J., deMan, A.-P. and Volberda, H.W. (2003), "Building alliance capability: management techniques for superior alliance performance", *Long Range Planning*, Vol. 36, No. 2, pp. 151-166.

Drucker, P.F. (1985), *Innovation and Entrepreneurship: Practices and Principles*, Harper & Row, New York.

Drucker, P.F. (1996), "Nonprofit prophet", *The Alliance Analyst*, available at: www.allianceanalyst.com.

Dudenhöffer, F. (2002), "On the structure of industries: findings from the automotive branch", *CAR – working paper*, No. 9, Rechklinghausen, pp. 1-17.

Dudenhöffer, F. (2003), "Gastkommentar: Was machen BMW und Mercedes besser?" [Guest commentary: What do BMW and Mercedes better?], *Automotive Engineering Partners*, No. 1, pp. 4.

Dull, S.F., Mohn, W.A. and Norén, T. (1995), "Partners", *The McKinsey Quarterly*, No. 4, pp. 63-72.

Dyer, J.H. (1996a), "Specialised supplier networks as a source of competitive advantage: evidence from the auto industry", *Strategic Management Journal*, Vol. 17, No. 4, pp. 271-291.

Dyer, J.H. (1996b), "How Chrysler created an American keiretsu", *Harvard Business Review*, July-August, pp. 42-56.

Dyer, J.H. (1996c), "Does governance matter? *Keiretsu* alliances and asset specificity as sources of Japanese competitive advantage", *Organization Science*, Vol. 7, No. 6, pp. 649-666.

Dyer, J.H. (1997), "Effective interfirm collaboration: How firms minimize transaction costs and maximize transaction value", *Strategic Management Journal*, Vol. 18, No. 7, pp. 535-556.

Dyer, J.H. (2000), *Collaborative Advantage: Winning through Extended Enterprise Supplier Networks,* Oxford University Press, New York.

Dyer, J.H. and Hatch, N.W. (2004), "Using supplier networks to learn faster", *MIT Sloan Management Review*, Spring, pp. 57-63.

Dyer, J.H. and Nobeoka, K. (2000), "Creating and managing a high-performance knowledge-sharing network: the Toyota case", *Strategic Management Journal*, Vol. 21, No. 3, pp. 345-367.

Dyer, J.H. and Ouchi, W.G. (1993), "Japanese-style partnerships: giving companies a competitive edge", *Sloan Management Review*, Fall, pp. 51-63.

Dyer, J.H. and Singh, H. (1998), "The relational view: cooperative strategy and sources of interorganizational competitive advantage", *Academy of Management Review,* Vol. 23, No. 4, pp. 660-679.

Dyer, J.H., Cho, D.S. and Chu, W. (1998), "Strategic supplier segmentation: the next 'best practice' in supply chain management", *California Management Review*, Vol. 40, No. 2, pp. 57-77.

Eccles, R.G. (1981), "The quasifirm in the construction industry", *Journal of Economic Behavior & Organization*, Vol. 2, No. 4, pp. 335-357.

Eisenhardt, K. (1989), "Building theories from case study research", *Academy of Management Review*, Vol. 14, No. 4, pp. 532-550.

Eisenhardt, K. (1991), "Better stories and better constructs: The case for rigor and comparative logic", *Academy of Management Review*, Vol. 16, No. 3, pp. 620-627.

Eisenhardt, K.M. and Martin, J. (2000), "Dynamic capabilities: what are they?", *Strategic Management Journal*, Vol. 21, Nos. 10/11, pp. 1105-1121.

Ellegaard, C. Johansen, J. and Drejer, A. (2003), "Managing industrial buyer-supplier relations – the case for attractiveness", *Integrated Manufacturing Systems*, Vol. 14, No. 4, pp. 346-356.

European Commission (2003), "Commission recommendation of 6 May 2003 concerning the definition of micro, small and medium-sized enterprises", *Official Journal of the European Union*, C(2003) 1422, L124/36-41.

Fine, C.H. (1998), *Clockspeed: Winning Industry Control in the Age of Temporary Advantage*, Perseus Books, New York.

Fine, C.H. (2000), "Clockspeed-based strategies for supply chain design", *Production and Operations Management*, Vol. 9, No. 3, pp. 213-221.

Fine, C.H., Vardan, R., Pethick, R. and El-Hout, J. (2002), "Rapid-response capability in value-chain design", *MIT Sloan Management Review*, Winter, pp. 69-75.

Forger, G. (2000), "Collaboration – the supply chain's defining factor?", *Supply Chain Management Review*, July-August, pp. 97-99.

Fritsch, M. and Lukas, R. (2001), "Who cooperates on R&D?", *Research Policy*, Vol. 30, No. 2, pp. 297-312.

Fynes, B., Voss, C. and de Búrca, S. (2005), "The impact of supply chain relationship quality on quality performance", *International Journal of Production Economics*, Vol. 96, No. 3, pp. 339-354.

Galunic, D.C. and Eisenhardt, K.M. (2001), "Architectural innovation and modular corporate forms", *Academy of Management Journal*, Vol. 44, No. 6, pp. 1229-1249.

Garel, G. and Midler, C. (2001), "Front-loading problem solving in co-development: managing the contractual, organizational and cognitive dimensions", *International Journal of Automotive Technology and Management*, Vol. 1, Nos. 2/3, pp. 236-251.

Geffen, C.A. and Rothenberg, S. (2000), "Suppliers and environmental innovation: the automotive paint process", *International Journal of Operations & Production Management*, Vol. 20, No. 2, pp. 166-186.

Gittell, J.H. and Weiss, L. (2004), "Coordination networks within and across organisations: a multi-level framework", *Journal of Management Studies*, Vol. 41, No. 1, pp. 127-153.

Glaser, B.G. (1978), *Theoretical Sensitivity*, Sociology Press, Mill Valley.

Glaser, B.G. (1994), "The constant comparative method of qualitative analysis", in Glaser, B.G. (Ed.), *More Grounded Theory Methodology: A Reader*, Sociology Press, Mill Valley, pp. 182-196.

Glaser, B.G. and Strauss, A.L. (1967), *The Discovery of Grounded Theory: Strategies for Qualitative Research*, Aldine, New York.

Glaser, B.G. and Strauss, A.L. (1971), "Discovery of substantive theory: A basic strategy underlying qualitative research", in: Filstead, W.J. (Ed.), *Qualitative Methodology: Firsthand Involvement with the Social World*. Markham Publishing, Chicago, pp. 288-304.

Goffin, K., Lemke, F. and Szwejczewski, M. (2006), "An exploratory study of 'close' supplier-manufacturer relationships", *Journal of Operations Management*, Vol. 24, No. 2, pp. 189-209.

Gomes-Casseres, B. (1994), "Group versus group: how alliance networks compete", *Harvard Business Review*, July – August, pp. 62-74

Gottschalk, B. (2001), "Die Deutsche Automobilzulieferindustrie – durch Innovationen zur Weltspitze" [The German automotive supplier industry – to the top of the world through innovation], *ZfAW*, No. 1, pp. 6-11.

Graham, G. and Ahmed, P. (2000), "Buyer-supplier management in the aerospace value chain", *Integrated Manufacturing Systems*, Vol. 11, No. 7, pp. 462-468.

Grandori, A. and Soda, G. (1995), "Inter-firm networks: antecedents, mechanisms and forms", *Organization Studies*, Vol. 16, No. 2, pp. 183-214.

Gulati, R. (1998), "Alliances and networks", *Strategic Management Journal*, Vol. 19, No. 4, pp. 293-317.

Gulati, R., Nohria, N. and Zaheer, A. (2000), "Strategic networks", *Strategic Management Journal*, Vol. 21, No. 3, pp. 203-215.

Hakansson, H. (1987), "Introduction", in Hakansson, H. (Ed.), *Industrial Technological Development: A Network Approach*, Croom Helm, London, pp. 3-25.

Hakansson, H. and Snehota, I. (1989), "No business is an island: the network concept of business strategy", *Scandinavian Journal of Management*, Vol. 5, No. 3, pp. 187-200.

Hakansson, P., Kjellberg, H. and Lundgren, A. (1993), "Strategic alliances in global biotechnology – a network approach", *International Business Review*, Vol. 2, No. 1, pp. 65-82.

Hallikas, J., Virolainen, V.-M. and Tuominen, M. (2002), "Understanding risk and uncertainty in supplier networks – a transaction cost approach", *International Journal of Production Research*, Vol. 40, No. 15, pp. 3519-3531.

Hamel, G. (1991), "Competition for competence and inter-partner learning within international strategic alliances", *Strategic Management Journal*, Vol. 12, Special Issue: Global Strategy, pp. 83-103.

Hamel, G. and Prahalad, C.K. (1994), *Competing for the Future*, Harvard Business School Press, Boston.

Hamel, G., Doz, Y.L. and Prahalad, C.K. (1989), "Collaborate with your competitors – and win", *Harvard Business Review*, January – February, pp. 133-139.

Handfield, R.B. and Bechtel, C. (2002), "The role of trust and relationship structure in improving supply chain responsiveness", *Industrial Marketing Management*, Vol. 31, No. 4, pp. 367-382.

Handfield, R.B. and Melnyk, S.A. (1998), "The scientific theory-building process: a primer using the case of TQM", *Journal of Operations Management*, Vol. 16, No. 4, pp. 321-339.

Harland, C.M. (1996), "Supply chain management: relationships, chain and networks", *British Journal of Management*, Vol. 7, Special Issue, pp. 63-80.

Harland, C.M. and Knight, L.A. (2001), "Supply network strategy: Role and competence requirements", *International Journal of Operations & Production Management*, Vol. 21, No. 4, pp. 476-489.

Harland, C.M., Brenchley, R. and Walker, H. (2003), "Risk in supply networks", *Journal of Purchasing & Supply Management*, Vol. 9, No. 2, pp. 51-62.

Harmsen, H., Grunert, K.G. and Bove, K. (2000), "Company competencies as a network: the role of product development", *Journal of Product Innovation Management*, Vol. 17, No. 3, pp. 194-207.

Hauschildt, J. (2004), *Innovationsmanagement* [Innovation Management], 3rd ed., Vahlen, München.

Hines, P. (1994), *Creating World Class Suppliers: Unlocking Mutual Competitive Advantage*, Pitman Publishing, London.

Hines, P. and Rich, N. (1997), "The seven value stream mapping tools", *International Journal of Operations & Production Management*, Vol. 17, No. 1, pp. 46-64.

Ho, D.C.K., Au, K.F. and Newton, E. (2002), "Empirical research on supply chain management: a critical review and recommendations", *International Journal of Production Research*, Vol. 40, No. 17, pp. 4415-4430.

Hult, G.T.M., Ketchen Jr., D.J., Cavusgil, S.T. and Calantone, R.J. (2006), "Knowledge as a strategic resource in supply chains", *Journal of Operations Management*, Vol. 24, No. 5, pp. 458-475.

Hurmelinna, P., Peltola, S., Tuimala, J. and Virolainen, V.-M. (2002), "Attaining world-class R&D by benchmarking buyer-supplier relationships", *International Journal of Production Economics*, Vol. 80, No. 1, pp. 39-47.

IBM (2006), "Expanding the innovation horizon", *The Global CEO Study 2006*, IBM Global Business Services, Somers.

Ilinitch, A.Y., D'Aveni, R.A. and Lewin, A.Y. (1996), "New organizational forms and strategies for managing in hypercompetitive environments", *Organization Science*, Vol. 7, No. 3, pp. 211-220.

Ireland, R.D., Hitt, M.A. and Vaidyanath, D. (2002), "Alliance management as a source of competitive advantage", *Journal of Management*, Vol. 28, No. 3, pp. 413-446.

Jacobides, M.G. and Winter, S.G. (2005), "The co-evolution of capabilities and transaction costs: explaining the institutional structure of production", *Strategic Management Journal*, Vol. 26, No. 5, pp. 395-413.

Jahn, H. (1988), *"Erzeugnisqualität, die logische Folge von Arbeitsqualität"* [Product quality, a logical consequence of work quality], VDI-Z, pp. 130-134.

Janda, S., Murray, J.B. and Burton , S. (2002), "Manufacturer-supplier relationships: An empirical test of a model of buyer outcomes", *Industrial Marketing Management*, Vol. 31, pp. 411-420.

Jarillo, J.C. (1988), "On strategic networks", *Strategic Management Journal*, Vol. 9, No. 1, pp. 31-41.

Jick, T.D. (1979), "Mixing qualitative and quantitative methods: Triangulation in action", *Administrative Science Quarterly*, Vol. 24, No. 4, pp. 602-611.

Johnsen, T. and Ford, D. (2005), "At the receiving end of supply network intervention: the view from an automotive first tier supplier", *Journal of Purchasing & Supply Management*, Vol. 11, No. 4, pp. 183-192.

Johnsen, T., Wynstra, F., Zheng, J., Harland, C. and Lamming, R. (2000), "Networking activities in supply networks", *Journal of Strategic Marketing*, Vol. 8, No. 2, pp. 161-181.

Johnston, D.A., McCutcheon, D.M., Stuart, F.I. and Kerwood, H. (2004), "Effects of supplier trust on performance of cooperative supplier relationships", *Journal of Operations Management*, Vol. 22, No. 1, pp. 23-38.

Jones, C., Hesterly, W.S. and Borgatti, S.P. (1997), "A general theory of network governance: exchange conditions and social mechanisms", *Academy of Management Review*, Vol. 22, No. 4, pp. 911-945.

Jürgens, U. (2000), "Towards new product and process development networks: the case of the German car industry", in Jürgens, U. (Ed.), *New Product Development and Production Networks*, Springer Verlag, Berlin, pp. 107-148.

Jürgens, U. (2004), "Characteristics of the European automotive system: is there a distinctive European approach?", *International Journal of Automotive Technology and Management*, Vol. 4, Nos. 2/3, pp. 112-136.

Kanter, R.M. (1994), "Collaborative advantage: the art of alliances", *Harvard Business Review*, July-August, pp. 96-108.

Kanter, R.M. (1999), "Change is everyone's job: managing the extended enterprise in a globally connected world", *Organizational Dynamics*, Vol. 28, No. 1, pp. 6-23.

Karlsson, C. (2003), "The development of industrial networks: challenges to operations management in an extraprise", *International Journal of Operations & Production Management*, Vol. 23, No. 1, pp. 44-61.

Katzensteiner, T. (2004), "Festgebissen" [Totally absorbed], *Wirtschaftswoche*, No. 50, 2.12.2004, pp. 66-68.

Kauffman, S. (1993), *The Origins of Order: Self-Organisation and Selection in Evolution*, Oxford University Press, Oxford.

Ketchen, D.J. and Giunipero, L.C. (2004), "The intersection of strategic management and supply chain management", *Industrial Marketing Management*, Vol. 33, No. 1, pp. 51-56.

Koehler, A. (2006), "Fliegende Autos" [Flying cars], *Wirtschaftswoche*, Nos. 1/2, 5.1.2006, pp. 36-42.

Kopczak, L.R. and Johnson, M.E. (2003), "The supply-chain management effect", *MIT Sloan Management Review*, Spring, pp. 27-34.

Kornelius, L. and Wamelink, J.W.F. (1998), "The virtual corporation: learning from construction", *Supply Chain Management: An International Journal*, Vol. 3, No. 4, pp. 193-202.

Kotler, P. (1997), *Marketing Management*, 9th ed., Prentice-Hall, Englewood Cliffs.

Koufteros, X., Vonderembse, M. and Jayaram, J. (2005), "Internal and external integration for product development: the contingency effects of uncertainty, equivocality, and platform strategy", *Decision Sciences*, Vol. 36, No. 1, pp. 97-133.

Kraljic, P. (1983), "Purchasing must become supply management", *Harvard Business Review*, September-October, pp. 109-117.

Krog, E. H. and Lochmahr, A. (2006): "Audi – a special report", *Automotive Logistics*, January/February 2005, pp. 66-69.

Kumar, N., Stern, L.W. and Anderson, J.C. (1993), "Conducting interorganizational research using key informants", *Academy of Management Journal*, Vol. 36, No. 6, pp. 1633-1651.

Kumar, S. and Seth, A. (1998), "The design of coordination and control mechanisms for managing joint venture-parent relationships", *Strategic Management Journal*, Vol. 19, No. 6, pp. 579-599.

Lakemond, N., Berggren, C. and Van Weele, A. (2006), "Coordinating supplier involvement in product development projects: a differentiated coordination typology", *R&D Management*, Vol. 36, No. 1, pp. 55-66.

Lambert, D.M., Emmelhainz, M.A. and Gardner, J.T. (1996), "Developing and implementing supply chain partnerships", *The International Journal of Logistics Management*, Vol. 7, No. 2, pp. 1–17.

Lamming, R. (2000), "Japanese supply chain relationships in recession", *Long Range Planning*, Vol. 33, No. 6, pp. 757-778.

Lamming, R.C., Johnsen, T., Zheng, J. and Harland, C. (2000), "An initial classification of supply networks", *International Journal of Operations & Production Management*, Vol. 20, No. 6, pp. 675-691.

Lawrence, T.B., Hardy, C. and Phillips, N. (2002), "Institutional effects of interorganizational collaboration: the emergence of proto-institutions", *Academy of Management Journal*, Vol. 45, No. 1, pp. 281-290.

Leary, M.R. (2001), *Introduction to Behavioral Research Methods*, 3rd ed., Allyn & Bacon, London.

Liedtka, J.M. (1999), "Linking competitive advantage with communities of practice", *Journal of Management Inquiry*, Vol. 8, No. 1, pp. 5-16.

Liker, J.K. and Choi, T.Y. (2004), "Building deep supplier relationships", *Harvard Business Review*, December, pp. 104-113.

Love, P.E.D., Li, H. and Mandal, P. (1999), "Rework: a symptom of a dysfunctional supply-chain", *European Journal of Purchasing & Supply Management*, Vol. 5, No. 1, pp. 1-11.

Luke, R.D., Begun, J.W. and Pointer, D.D. (1989), "Quasi firms: strategic interorganizational forms in the health care industry", *Academy of Management Review*, Vol. 14, No. 1, pp. 9-19.

Mabert, V.A. and Venkataramanan, M.A. (1998), "Special research focus on supply chain linkages: challenges for design and management in the 21st century", *Decision Sciences*, Vol. 29, No. 3, pp. 537-552.

MacBeth, D.K. (2002), "Emergent strategy in managing cooperative supply chain change", *International Journal of Operations & Production Management*, Vol. 22, No. 7, pp. 728- 740.

MacBeth, D.K. and Ferguson (1994), *Partnership Sourcing: an Integrated Supply Chain Management Approach*, Pitman Publishing, London.

Madhavan, R., Koka, B.R. and Prescott, J.E. (1998), "Networks in transition: how industry events (re)shape interfirm relationships", *Strategic Management Journal*, Vol. 19, No. 5, pp. 439-459.

Madhok, A. and Tallman, S.B. (1998), "Resources, transactions and rents: managing value through interfirm collaborative relationships", *Organization Science*, Vol. 9, No. 3, pp. 326-339.

Magretta, J. (1998), "The power of virtual integration: an interview with Dell Computer's Micheal Dell", *Harvard Business Review*, Vol. 76, March-April, pp. 73-84.

Maloni, M. and Benton, W.C. (2000), "Power influences in the supply chain", *Journal of Business Logistics*, Vol. 21, No. 1, pp. 49-73.

March J.G. (1991), "Exploration and exploitation in organizational learning", *Organization Science*, Vol. 2, No. 1, pp. 71–87.

Martínez Sánchez, A. and Pérez Pérez, M. (2003), "Cooperation and the ability to minimize the time and cost of new product development within the Spanish automotive supplier industry", *Journal of Product Innovation Management*, Vol. 20, No. 1, pp. 57-69.

Martinez, M.T., Fouletier, P. Park. K.H. and Favrel, J. (2001), "Virtual enterprise – organisation, evolution and control", *International Journal of Production Economics*, Vol. 74, Nos. 1-3, pp. 225-238.

McCutcheon, D.M. and Meredith, J.R. (1993), Conducting case study research in operations management, *Journal of Operations Management*, Vol. 11, No. 3, pp. 239-256.

McFarlan, F. W. and Nolan, R. L. (1995), "How to manage an IT outsourcing alliance", *Sloan Management Review*, Winter, pp. 9-23.

McHugh, P., Merli, G. and Wheeler, G. III (1995), *Beyond Business Process Reengineering*, Wiley, Chichester.

McIvor, R. (2000), "A practical framework for understanding the outsourcing process", *Supply Chain Management: An International Journal*, Vol. 5, No. 1, pp. 22-36.

Mentzer, J.T., DeWitt, W., Keebler, J.S., Min, S., Nix, N.W., Smith, C.D. and Zacharia, Z.G. (2001), "Defining supply chain management", *Journal of Business Logistics*, Vol. 22, No. 2, pp. 1-25.

Mercer Management Consulting (2004), "Future Automotive Industry Structure (FAST) 2015", *Study*, München.

Mikkola, J.H. (2003), "Modularity, component outsourcing, and inter-firm learning", *R&D Management*, Vol. 33, No. 4, pp. 439-454.

Miles, R.E. and Snow, C.C. (1986), "Organizations: new concepts for new forms", *California Management Review*, Vol. 28, Spring, pp. 62-73.

Mills, J., Schmitz, J. and Frizelle, G. (2004), "A strategic review of 'supply networks'", *International Journal of Operations & Production Management*, Vol. 24, No. 10, pp. 1012-1036.

Min, S. and Mentzer, J.T. (2000), "The role of marketing in supply chain management", *International Journal of Physical Distribution & Logistics Management*, Vol. 30, No. 9, pp. 765-787.

Mintzberg, H., Ahlstrand, B. and Lampel, J. (1998), *Strategy Safari: A Guided Tour through the Wilds of Strategic Management*, Simon & Schuster, New York.

Miotti, L. and Sachwald, F. (2003), "Cooperative R&D: why and with whom? An integrated framework of analysis", *Research Policy*, Vol. 32, No. 8, pp. 1481-1499.

Mohr, J. and Spekman, R. (1994), "Characteristics of partnership success: partnership attributes, communication behavior, and conflict resolution techniques", *Strategic Management Journal*, Vol. 15, No. 2, pp. 135-152.

Möller, K.E. and Svahn, S. (2003), "Managing strategic nets: a capability perspective", *Marketing Theory*, Vol. 3, No. 2, pp. 209-234.

Monczka, R.M., Petersen, K.J., Handfield, R.B. and Ragatz, G.L. (1998), "Success factors in strategic supplier alliances: the buying company perspective", *Decision Sciences*, Vol. 29, No. 3, pp. 553-577.

Morris, D. (1969), *The Human Zoo*, Jonathan Cape, London.

Morton, S.C., Dainty, A.R.J., Burns, N.D., Brookes, N.J. and Backhouse, C.J. (2006), "Managing relationships to improve performance: a case study in the global aerospace industry", *International Journal of Production Research*, Vol. 44, No. 16, pp. 3227-3241.

Narasimhan, R. and Nair, A. (2005), "The antecedent role of quality, information sharing and supply chain proximity on strategic alliance formation and performance", *International Journal of Production Economics*, Vol. 96, No. 3, pp. 301-313.

Nassimbeni, G. (1998), "Network structures and co-ordination mechanisms: a taxonomy"; *International Journal of Operations & Production Management*, Vol. 18, No. 6, pp. 538-554.

Nellore, R. and Söderquist, K. (2000), "Portfolio approaches to procurement: analysing the missing link to specifications", *Long Range Planning*, Vol. 33, No. 2, pp. 245-267.

Noori, H. and Lee, W.B. (2004), "Collaborative design in a networked enterprise: the case of the telecommunication industry", *International Journal of Production Research*, Vol. 42, No. 15, pp. 3041-3054.

Obstfeld, D. (2005), "Social networks, the *tertius iungens* orientation, and involvement in innovation", *Administrative Science Quarterly*, Vol. 50, No. 1, pp. 100-130.

Olsen, R.F. and Ellram, L.M. (1997a), "Buyer-supplier relationships: alternative research approaches", *European Journal of Purchasing & Supply Management*, Vol. 3, No. 4, pp. 221-231.

Olsen, R.F. and Ellram, L.M. (1997b), "A portfolio approach to supplier relationships", *Industrial Marketing Management*, Vol. 26, No. 2, pp. 101-113.

Otto, A. and Kotzab, H. (2003), "Does supply chain management really pay? Six perspectives to measure the performance of managing a supply chain", *European Journal of Operational Research*, Vol. 144, No. 2, pp. 306-320.

Ouchi, W.G. (1980), "Markets, bureaucracies, and clans", *Administrative Science Quarterly*, Vol. 25, No. 1, pp. 129-142.

Parry, G. and Graves, A. (2008), Build to Order: The Road to the 5 Day Car, Springer, London 2008.

Petersen, K.J., Handfield, R.B. and Ragatz, G.L. (2005), "Supplier integration into new product development: coordinating product, process and supply chain design", *Journal of Operations Management*, Vol. 23, Nos. 3/4, pp. 371-388.

Petroni, A. and Panciroli, B. (2002), "Innovation as a determinant of suppliers' roles and performances: an empirical study in the food machinery industry", *European Journal of Purchasing & Supply Management*, Vol. 8, No. 3, pp. 135-149.

Pettigrew, A.M. (1990), "Longitudinal field research on change: Theory and practice", *Organization Science*, Vol. 1, No. 3, pp. 267-292.

Pfeffer, J. and Salancik, G.R. (1978), *The External Control of Organizations: A Resource Dependency Perspective*, Harper & Row, New York.

Powell, W.W. (1998), "Learning from collaboration: knowledge and networks in the biotechnology and pharmaceutical industries", *California Management Review*, Vol. 40, No. 3, pp. 228-240.

Powell, W.W., Koput, K.W. and Smith-Doerr, L. (1996), "Interorganizational collaboration and the locus of innovation: networks of learning in biotechnology", *Administrative Science Quarterly*, Vol. 41, No. 1, pp. 116-145.

Prahalad, C.K. and Hamel, G. (1990), The core competence of the corporation", *Harvard Business Review*, May, pp. 79-91.

Prajogo, D.I. and Sohal, A.S. (2006), "The integration of TQM and technology/R&D management in determining quality and innovation performance", *OMEGA – The International Journal of Management Science*, Vol. 34, No. 3, pp. 296-312.

Price, H. (1996), "The anthropology of the supply chain: Fiefs, clans, witch-doctors and professors", *European Journal of Purchasing & Supply Management*, Vol. 2, Nos. 2/3, pp. 87-105.

Primo, M.A.M. and Amundson, S.D. (2002), "An exploratory study of the effects of supplier relationships on new product development outcomes", *Journal of Operations Management*, Vol. 20, No. 1, pp. 33-52.

Proff, H. (2000), "Hybrid strategies as a strategic challenge – the case of the German automotive industry", *OMEGA – The International Journal of Management Science*, Vol. 28, No. 5, pp. 541-553.

Quinn, J.B. (2000), "Outsourcing innovation: the new engine of growth", *Sloan Management Review*, Summer, pp. 13-28.

Quinn, J.B. and Hilmer, F.G. (1994), "Strategic outsourcing", *Sloan Management Review*, Summer, pp. 43-55.

Ritter, T. (1999), "The networking company: antecedents for coping with relationships and networks effectively", *Industrial Marketing Management*, Vol. 28, No. 5, pp, 467-479.

Ritter, T. and Gemünden, H.G. (2003), "Interorganizational relationships and networks: an overview", *Journal of Business Research*, Vol. 56, No. 9, pp. 691-697.

Roland Berger Strategy Consultants (1999), "Eight mega-trends re-shaping the automotive supplier industry – a trend study to 2010", *Study*, München.

Rommel, G.K., Kempis, R.D. and Kaas, H.W. (1994), "Does quality pay?"; *The McKinsey Quarterly*, No. 1, pp. 51-63.

Rossetti, C. and Choi, T.Y. (2005), "On the dark side of strategic sourcing: experiences from the aerospace industry", *Academy of Management Executive*, Vol. 19, No. 1, pp. 46-60.

Sampler, J. L. (1998), "Redefining industry structure for the information age", *Strategic Management Journal*, Vol. 19, No. 4, pp. 343-355.

Savage, C.M. (1990), *Fifth Generation Management*, Digital Press, Woburn.

Schilling, M.A. and Steensma, H.K. (2001), "The use of modular organizational forms: an industry-level analysis", *Academy of Management Journal*, Vol. 44, No. 6, pp. 1149-1168.

Schumpeter, J.A. (1934), *Theorie der wirtschaftlichen Entwicklung* [The theory of economic development], 4th ed., Duncker und Humblot, Berlin.

Singh, P.J., Smith, A. and Sohal, A.S. (2005), "Strategic supply chain management issues in the automotive industry: an Australian perspective", *International Journal of Production Research*, Vol. 43, No. 16, pp. 3375-3399.

Smith, A. (1776), *The Wealth of Nations*, Reprint: 1982, Penguin Books, New York.

Snow, C.C. and Thomas, J.B. (1994), "Field research methods in strategic management. Contributions to theory building and testing", *Journal of Management Studies*, Vol. 31, No. 4, pp. 457-480.

Snow, C.C., Miles, R.E. and Coleman Jr., H.J. (1992), "Managing 21st century network organisations", *Organizational Dynamics*, Winter, pp. 5-20.

Stake, R.E. (1995), *The Art of Case Study Research*, Sage, Thousand Oaks.

Strauss, A.L. (1987), *Qualitative Analysis for Social Scientists*, Cambridge University Press, Cambridge.

Strauss, A.L. and Corbin, J. (1998), *Basics of Qualitative Research: Grounded Theory Procedures and Techniques*, 2nd ed., Sage, Thousand Oaks.

Suddaby, R. (2006), "From the editors: what grounded theory is not", *Academy of Management Journal*, Vol. 49, No. 4, pp. 633-642.

Svensson, G. (2003), "Holistic and cross-disciplinary deficiencies in the theory generation of supply chain management", *Supply Chain Management: An International Journal*, Vol. 8, No. 4, pp. 303-316.

Svensson, G. (2004), "Supplier segmentation in the automotive industry: a dyadic approach of a managerial model", *International Journal of Physical Distribution & Logistics Management*, Vol. 34, No. 1, pp. 12-38.

Swink, M.L. and Mabert, V.A. (2000), "Product development partnerships: balancing the needs of OEMs and suppliers", *Business Horizons*, May-June, pp. 59-68.

Sydow, J. (1992), *Strategische Netzwerke: Evolution und Organisation* [Strategic networks: evolution and organisation], Gabler, Wiesbaden.

Thorelli, H.B. (1986), "Networks: between markets and hierarchies", *Strategic Management Journal*, Vol. 7, No. 1, pp. 37-51.

Trienekens, J.H. and Beulens, A.J.M. (2001), "View on inter-enterprise relationships", *Production Planning & Control*, Vol. 12, No. 5, pp. 466-477.

Ulrich, K.T. and Eppinger, S.D. (1995), *Product Design and Development*, McGraw-Hill, New York.

Usdiken, B., Sozen, Z. and Enbiyaoglu, H. (1988), "Strategies and boundaries: subcontracting in construction", *Strategic Management Journal*, Vol. 9, No. 6, pp. 633-637.

Van der Valk, W. and Wynstra, F. (2005), "Supplier involvement in new product development in the food industry", *Industrial Marketing Management*, Vol. 34, No. 7, pp. 681-694.

Vastag, G. and Montabon, F. (2002), "Journal characteristics, rankings and social acculturation in operations management", *OMEGA – The International Journal of Management Science*, Vol. 30, No. 2, pp. 109-126.

VDA (2006), *Annual Report 2006*, Verband der Deutschen Automobilindustrie, Frankfurt.

Von Corswant, F. and Fredriksson, P. (2002), "Sourcing trends in the car industry – a survey of car manufacturers' and suppliers' strategies and relations", *International Journal of Operations & Production Management*, Vol. 22, No. 7, pp. 741-758.

Vonderembse, M.A., Uppal, M., Huang, S.H. and Dismukes, J.P. (2006), "Designing supply chains: towards theory development", *International Journal of Production Economics*, Vol. 100, No. 2, pp. 223-238.

Voss, C. (1995), "Operations management - from Taylor to Toyota – and beyond", *British Journal of Management*, Vol. 6, No. 6, pp. 17-30.

Wagner, S.M. and Hoegl, M. (2006), "Involving suppliers in product development: insights from R&D directors and project managers", *Industrial Marketing Management*, Vol. 35, No. 8, pp. 936-943.

Walters, D. (2004), "New economy – new business models – new approaches", *International Journal of Physical Distribution & Logistics Management*, Vol. 34, Nos. 3/4, pp. 219-229.

Weisenfeld, U., Reeves, J.C. and Hunck-Meiswinkel, A. (2001), "Technology management and collaboration profile: virtual companies and industrial platforms in the high-tech biotechnology industries", *R&D Management*, Vol. 31, No. 1, pp. 91-100.

Wernerfelt, B. (1984), "A resource-based view of the firm", *Strategic Management Journal*, Vol. 5, No. 2, pp. 171-180.

Williamson, O.E. (1975), *Market and Hierarchies: Analysis and Antitrust Implications*, Free Press, New York.

Wolters, H. and Schuller, F. (1997), "Explaining supplier-buyer partnerships: a dynamic game theory approach", *European Journal of Purchasing & Supply Management*, Vol. 3, No. 3, pp. 155-164.

Womack, J.P. and Jones, D.T. (1994), "From lean production to the lean enterprise", *Harvard Business Review*, March-April, pp. 93-103.

Wood, D.J. and Gray, B. (1991), "Toward a comprehensive theory of collaboration", *Journal of Applied Behavioral Science*, Vol. 27, No. 2, pp. 139-162.

Wynstra, F. and Pierick, E. ten (2000), "Managing supplier involvement in new product development: a portfolio approach", *European Journal of Purchasing & Supply Management*, Vol. 6, No. 1, pp. 49-57.

Yin, R.K. (2003), *Case Study Research: Design and Methods*, Applied social research methods series. Vol. 5, 3rd ed., Sage, Beverly Hills.

Zirpoli, F. and Caputo, M. (2002), "The nature of buyer-supplier relationships in co-design activities: the Italian auto industry case", *International Journal of Operations & Production Management*, Vol. 22, No. 12, pp. 1389-1410.

APPENDIX

APPENDIX A: INTERVIEW GUIDE

Interview Guide

The study underlying this interview explores how future organisational structures (networks of companies) in the automotive industry can gain competitive advantage within their industry by efficiently exploiting inter-organisational collaborations based on a new governance architectures.

The interview is semi-structured and should not exceed 1.5 to 2 hours in total. The following is a set of typical questions on various topics, which does not represent an exclusive catalogue but has enough structure to reveal the necessary data. This should enable both parties (the interviewee as well as the interviewer) to expand and adapt questions within the given topics.

Section 1: Industrial context

- Industrial environment
    - Current industrial landscape
        - Major constraints
        - Company's reaction
    - Main players and distribution of power among them
        - Customers
        - Competitors
        - Suppliers
        - Role of the company itself

- Changes over the past
  - Reasons / causes
  - Drivers / Responsibilities (Who, What)
  - Objectives (cost, quality, efficiency, responsiveness, other)
  - Company's adaptation
- Future trends
  - Reasons / causes
  - Drivers / Responsibilities (Who, What)
  - Objectives
  - Company's possible reaction
- Ideal situation

Section 2: Company context

- Basic background

  - Company figures
  - Strategic goals
  - Product and services (market segments → premium)

- Describe the basis upon which you deliver products and services (e.g. quality, speed, flexibility, dependability, cost, range, others)
- How does this deliver value to your customers / why would they choose you
- Depending on different types of projects are different aspects important
- How does it enable you to differentiate from your competitors
- Would you consider these as your core competencies
- Why is it a core competence rather than a support function
- What specifies a core competence to you
- How did you develop your competencies
- What opportunities do they give you for the future
- What are possible threats to your competencies
- How important are competencies for business in automotive sector
- Does competence determine strategy or vice versa

Section 3: Collaboration in R&D context

- Value system in joint R&D and product development

    - Process steps
    - Participants / value members
    - Contribution of participants

- Considering outsourcing of business to suppliers

    - What are your main reasons / motives for outsourcing and collaboration
    - What are your individual experiences
    - How does outsourcing impact on relationship (e.g. are suppliers more integrated)

- On which basis are suppliers selected / on which basis do you think the OEM selects its suppliers
- When do you consider a supplier / partner to be the most competent one
- How does the nomination and selection process look like

    - What sort of data do you use / is there a classification framework (ABC supplier, etc.)
    - In what way do you use the data
    - Does it have particular influence on the selection of suppliers
    - Is there a relation between certain customer requirements and the selection of suppliers
    - If yes, how does the general causality look like
    - Is there a standardised approach

- What risks are involved in selecting the right supplier
- Database
- How can collaboration between OEM and supplier be characterised

    - What are the basic collaborative steps in a project
    - How close would you evaluate your collaborative relationship (e.g. degree of integration, involvement, etc.)

- Does partnership exist on the organisational level and not only on personal one
- How do you perceive the negotiations / how are decisions made
- How deep is supplier involved in the learning process of the OEM
- How are resources shared (e.g. tools, processes, etc.)
- How does it impact on competence development and deployment
- What are main challenges / difficulties in collaborating

    - Reasons
    - How to solve it

- What effect does IT have in this
- Does the industry landscape aid or constrain this
- Does the 'Lopes-effect' still have an impact

- What makes a good collaboration for you
- What benefits would you expect of collaboration
- What was the evolutionary development of your collaborative activities

    - Stages
    - Drivers / responsibilities (who, what)
    - Objectives (cost, quality, efficiency, responsiveness, other)
    - Necessary effort /commitment

- What has changed because of collaboration

    - Results (customer satisfaction, speed, efficiency, flexibility, new positions created, others)
    - Effects on company (organisational culture, way of working, etc.)
    - Effects on industry landscape

- Has there been a particular effect on the success of the company
    - Measurement (how do you measure success)

Section 4: Stories and narratives

- Please give any good examples of the issues discussed above.

APPENDIX B: QUESTIONNAIRE

Instructions

In the following questionnaire, a number of statements about inter-organisational collaboration in the automotive industry will be presented to you. It is your task to assess each statement based on your practical experience by measuring:

AGREEMENT: State how strongly you agree or disagree with the statement using the given scale from 'strongly agree' to 'strongly disagree'.

IMPORTANCE: State how important you think the statement is for your daily business operations using the given scale from 'Very high' to 'Very low'.

For each dimension please tick one box only! There are no right and wrong answers. Please evaluate the statements as honestly and openly as you can. At the end, a brief section on demographical information is also included.

An example for illustration is given below.

0	Private businesses must make profit				

AGREEMENT	Strongly agree	Agree	Neutral	Disagree	Strongly disagree
	X				
IMPORTANCE	Very high	High	Medium	Low	Very low
	X				

We very much appreciate your help
THANK YOU!

STATEMENTS

1	Change in the automotive industry is driven by a combination of general industrial forces and internal company issues				
AGREEMENT	Strongly agree	Agree	Neutral	Disagree	Strongly disagree
IMPORTANCE	Very high	High	Medium	Low	Very low

2	Increasing complexity, cost pressure and shorter product development lead times have led to more inter-firm collaboration based on product modularisation				
AGREEMENT	Strongly agree	Agree	Neutral	Disagree	Strongly disagree
IMPORTANCE	Very high	High	Medium	Low	Very low

3	Car manufacturer are changing their adversarial pricing policies in supplier selection towards more strategic sourcing policies				
AGREEMENT	Strongly agree	Agree	Neutral	Disagree	Strongly disagree
IMPORTANCE	Very high	High	Medium	Low	Very low

4	The challenge for a collaborative supply network is to maintain competitiveness without applying adversarial forces				
AGREEMENT	Strongly agree	Agree	Neutral	Disagree	Strongly disagree
IMPORTANCE	Very high	High	Medium	Low	Very low

5	Focusing on core competencies is becoming increasingly important in order to drive the development and management of inter-firm collaboration in the supply network				
AGREEMENT	Strongly agree	Agree	Neutral	Disagree	Strongly disagree
IMPORTANCE	Very high	High	Medium	Low	Very low

6	Structure of the supply network is determined by the strategy of the car manufacturer				
AGREEMENT	Strongly agree	Agree	Neutral	Disagree	Strongly disagree
IMPORTANCE	Very high	High	Medium	Low	Very low

7	Product modularisation affects how a supply network is structured				
AGREEMENT	Strongly agree	Agree	Neutral	Disagree	Strongly disagree
IMPORTANCE	Very high	High	Medium	Low	Very low

8	Different relationships and collaborative practices exist for different inter-company (car manufacturer and supplier) projects in the supply network				
AGREEMENT	Strongly agree	Agree	Neutral	Disagree	Strongly disagree
IMPORTANCE	Very high	High	Medium	Low	Very low

9	The role of an organisation in the supply network is mainly determined by what competencies are offered by it				
AGREEMENT	Strongly agree	Agree	Neutral	Disagree	Strongly disagree
IMPORTANCE	Very high	High	Medium	Low	Very low

10	The role of an organisation in the supply network is partly determined by the stages of the product development process				
AGREEMENT	Strongly agree	Agree	Neutral	Disagree	Strongly disagree
IMPORTANCE	Very high	High	Medium	Low	Very low

11	Relationships between companies in the supply network change over time				
AGREEMENT	Strongly agree	Agree	Neutral	Disagree	Strongly disagree
IMPORTANCE	Very high	High	Medium	Low	Very low

12	An individual company can collaborate in more than one project within the supply network at the same time				
AGREEMENT	Strongly agree	Agree	Neutral	Disagree	Strongly disagree
IMPORTANCE	Very high	High	Medium	Low	Very low

13	An inter-firm collaboration in the supply network needs to be formed on the basis of technical competencies and mutual exchange of knowledge				
AGREEMENT	Strongly agree	Agree	Neutral	Disagree	Strongly disagree
IMPORTANCE	Very high	High	Medium	Low	Very low

14	There is the need for a coordinator and leader within the supply network that has the competence to evaluate and manage the interfaces in a collaboration				
AGREEMENT	Strongly agree	Agree	Neutral	Disagree	Strongly disagree
IMPORTANCE	Very high	High	Medium	Low	Very low

15	The co-ordinator of the supply network should have its own core competencies and encourage those of other organisations to participate				
AGREEMENT	Strongly agree	Agree	Neutral	Disagree	Strongly disagree
IMPORTANCE	Very high	High	Medium	Low	Very low

16	Competencies of separate organisations participating in a collaboration within the supply network need to be linked via cross-company project infrastructures				
AGREEMENT	Strongly agree	Agree	Neutral	Disagree	Strongly disagree
IMPORTANCE	Very high	High	Medium	Low	Very low

17	Different projects in the supply network have to be managed differently				
AGREEMENT	Strongly agree	Agree	Neutral	Disagree	Strongly disagree
IMPORTANCE	Very high	High	Medium	Low	Very low

18	Overly stable relationships between companies in the supply network can lead to a loss of innovativeness				
AGREEMENT	Strongly agree	Agree	Neutral	Disagree	Strongly disagree
IMPORTANCE	Very high	High	Medium	Low	Very low

19	New inter-firm collaborations produce innovative solutions				
AGREEMENT	Strongly agree	Agree	Neutral	Disagree	Strongly disagree
IMPORTANCE	Very high	High	Medium	Low	Very low

20	Car manufacturers still retain overall responsibility for the management of the whole supply network				
AGREEMENT	Strongly agree	Agree	Neutral	Disagree	Strongly disagree
IMPORTANCE	Very high	High	Medium	Low	Very low

21	To become more influential in the supply network a company must take responsibility for integrating other companies and their products				
AGREEMENT	Strongly agree	Agree	Neutral	Disagree	Strongly disagree
IMPORTANCE	Very high	High	Medium	Low	Very low

22	Early and intense integration of strategic collaborators facilitates the successful delivery of a project				
AGREEMENT	Strongly agree	Agree	Neutral	Disagree	Strongly disagree
IMPORTANCE	Very high	High	Medium	Low	Very low

23	At early stages of the collaboration process technical and social rather than monetary aspects have to be measured and compared				
AGREEMENT	Strongly agree	Agree	Neutral	Disagree	Strongly disagree
IMPORTANCE	Very high	High	Medium	Low	Very low

24	Strategic and long term thinking for the whole supply network increases the chance of successful inter-firm collaboration				
AGREEMENT	Strongly agree	Agree	Neutral	Disagree	Strongly disagree
IMPORTANCE	Very high	High	Medium	Low	Very low

25	The boundaries of responsibilities between collaborating parties need to be clearly defined to deliver a successful inter-firm project within the supply network				
AGREEMENT	Strongly agree	Agree	Neutral	Disagree	Strongly disagree
IMPORTANCE	Very high	High	Medium	Low	Very low

26	Functional and short-term thinking within an organisation produces sub-optimisation for the supply network				
AGREEMENT	Strongly agree	Agree	Neutral	Disagree	Strongly disagree
IMPORTANCE	Very high	High	Medium	Low	Very low

27	The existence of cross-functional units that can act autonomously from other parts of the same company facilitate inter-firm collaboration				
AGREEMENT	Strongly agree	Agree	Neutral	Disagree	Strongly disagree
IMPORTANCE	Very high	High	Medium	Low	Very low

28	To operate autonomously within the organisation and to integrate in the supply network cross-functional units must have both unique resources and interface capabilities				
AGREEMENT	Strongly agree	Agree	Neutral	Disagree	Strongly disagree
IMPORTANCE	Very high	High	Medium	Low	Very low

29	The more mature, attractive and transferable a competence is the more potential value it can create for the supply network				
AGREEMENT	Strongly agree	Agree	Neutral	Disagree	Strongly disagree
IMPORTANCE	Very high	High	Medium	Low	Very low

30	Competencies can be developed and deployed through collaboration with other companies in the supply network				
AGREEMENT	Strongly agree	Agree	Neutral	Disagree	Strongly disagree
IMPORTANCE	Very high	High	Medium	Low	Very low

31	For each new inter-firm project a new appropriate supply base has to be selected and managed				
AGREEMENT	Strongly agree	Agree	Neutral	Disagree	Strongly disagree
IMPORTANCE	Very high	High	Medium	Low	Very low

32	There is a positive correlation between the extent of inter-firm collaboration and the sustainable success of the supply network and its individual companies				
AGREEMENT	Strongly agree	Agree	Neutral	Disagree	Strongly disagree
IMPORTANCE	Very high	High	Medium	Low	Very low

33	Establishing inter-firm collaboration is an effective way of improving quality and innovation of products as well as reducing development lead-times and cost in a supply network				
AGREEMENT	Strongly agree	Agree	Neutral	Disagree	Strongly disagree
IMPORTANCE	Very high	High	Medium	Low	Very low

34	The short term success of inter-firm collaboration in the supply network is related to cost and lead time reduction				
AGREEMENT	Strongly agree	Agree	Neutral	Disagree	Strongly disagree
IMPORTANCE	Very high	High	Medium	Low	Very low

35	The long term success of inter-firm collaboration in the supply network is related to quality and innovation improvement				
AGREEMENT	Strongly agree	Agree	Neutral	Disagree	Strongly disagree
IMPORTANCE	Very high	High	Medium	Low	Very low

DEMOGRAPHICS

1. Have you been participating in the interviews? (Please tick one box only)

YES	
NO	

2. How long have you been working in the automotive industry? (Please indicate figure)

YEARS	

3. Which type(s) of company have you had experience working in? (Please tick as many boxes as appropriate)

CAR MANUFACTURER	
SYSTEMS SUPPLIER	
MODULE SUPPLIER	
PART / COMPONENT SUPPLIER	
ASSEMBLY SERVICE PROVIDER	
LOGISTICS SERVICE PROVIDER	
ENGINEERING SERVICE PROVIDER	
OTHER (PLEASE SPECIFY)	

4. Approximately how big is the company you are working for now? (Please indicate figures)

EMPLOYEES	
TURNOVER	

5. In which function(s) have you had experience working in? (Please tick as many boxes as appropriate)

R&D / STYLING	
PURCHASING	
QUALITY ASSURANCE	
PRODUCTION / MANUFACTURING	
LOGISTICS	
MARKETING / SALES	
STRATEGY / DIRECTORSHIP	
OTHER (PLEASE SPECIFY)	

6. What organisational responsibility level do you currently occupy? (Please tick one box only)

CLERK LEVEL	
JUNIOR MANAGEMENT LEVEL	
MIDDLE MANAGEMENT LEVEL	
SENIOR MANEGEMENT LEVEL	
TOP MANAGEMENT / EXECUTIVE LEVEL	
OTHER (PLEASE SPECIFY)	

We very much appreciate your help – **THANK YOU!**

INDEX

U

T

V

W

Y